SAVING CHRISTIANITY

SAVING CHRISTIANITY

New Thinking for Old Beliefs

Hilary Wakeman

With a Foreword by Bishop Willie Walsh

The Liffey Press

Published by
The Liffey Press Ltd
Ashbrook House, 10 Main Street
Raheny, Dublin 5, Ireland
www.theliffeypress.com

A catalogue record of this book is
available from the British Library.

ISBN 1-904148-32-8

Printed in the Republic of Ireland by Colour Books Ltd.

CONTENTS

ABOUT THE AUTHOR

Hilary Wakeman was among the first women ordained as priest in the Church of England, in 1994. She was working in the Church, as deaconess and then deacon, for nine years prior to that, and was one of the few to be in charge of a parish while still a deacon. She was a member of the General Synod, the Church of England's governing body, from 1990 to 1995, and was made an Honorary Canon of Norwich Cathedral in 1994. In 1996 she became Rector of a Church of Ireland parish in County Cork.

In 1973, Hilary founded an ecumenical network of groups practising Christian meditation, or contemplative prayer, at a time when she was a housewife and mother of five young children. Known as the Julian Meetings, the network is now worldwide. She is still its Convenor.

After leaving school at sixteen, she worked in public libraries and then as a journalist and broadcaster, in England and in the USA. From 1984 to 1988, while completing her theological training, she was the acting Communications Officer for Norwich Diocese.

Hilary retired from parish ministry in 2001; she and her husband continue to live in Ireland, where they edit *The SHOp*, a much-acclaimed poetry magazine. She also edits *Le Chéile*, a small "newsletter of hope for Christianity in Ireland", and chairs the steering group of the Progressive Christianity Network, Ireland.

Previous publications include *Women Priests: The First Years* (Darton Longman & Todd, 1996) and *Circles of Stillness: Thoughts on Contemplative Prayer from the Julian Meetings* (Darton Longman & Todd, 2002).

FOREWORD

I read much of this book travelling by air from Rome to Dublin. I had just attended a three-day Conference of Bishops where our beliefs were secure and unquestioned. I was returning to Dublin where, at this time, much of what we were taking for granted in Rome is being questioned and sometimes rejected.

I found Hilary Wakeman's *Saving Christianity* disturbing. Was it leading me from Rome to Dublin, persuading me to question some of the beliefs which I have always held sacred and unchanging?

One of the central themes of this book is that we need to discuss our Christian belief if "moderate Christianity" is to survive. She argues that we need to find new ways of expressing old truths. One can hardly disagree with the thrust of this approach. Indeed, I am mindful of Pope John XXIII speaking on a similar fashion at the opening of the Second Vatican Council.

Hilary Wakeman in her search goes *beyond* finding new ways of expressing old truths. It seems to me in some cases she concludes that the old truth is simply not true, and this I find disturbing.

Disturbing, yes, but always engaging. I found myself agreeing with many of her conclusions — the need to recognise all that the various world religious share, that Jew and Muslim, Christian, Hindu and Buddhist worship the same God and that we hardly do justice to that God by limiting Him to our small vision. I found myself in sharp disagreement with others — her interpretation of the Resurrection stories and of course the very basic question of who is Jesus.

This is a profound and scholarly book, based on an impressive range of theological study. Yet it is also a simple and readable book which uses the author's own lived experience and significant clarity of thought to explain her beliefs.

Hilary Wakeman asks many questions that some of us dare not ask and yet it is surely only through prayerful reflection and courageous struggling with our doubts and questions that we can seek a faith which allows us to live with integrity. It is only by being honest and indeed loving in our agreements and disagreements that we can continue to search for and work towards that unity in diversity which all genuinely religious people feel the need to pursue.

Hilary Wakeman's book challenges all of us to be courageous, honest and loving. I am grateful to her for challenging me to try to be courageous, honest and loving in writing a Foreword to this book.

✝ Willie Walsh
R.C. Bishop of Killaloe

"We do not know what God is." — *St Thomas Aquinas*

"If you understand, then it is not God." — *St Augustine*

"What is demanded is only your being open and willing to accept what is given to you, the New Being, the being of love and justice and truth, as it is manifest in Him whose yoke is easy and whose burden is light." — *Paul Tillich*

"There is the danger of a rethinking of Christianity which is so radical that the product is no longer Christian. And there is the danger of a failure to rethink which results in Christianity becoming a specialised interest of the few, wrapped in an out-moded world-view which is increasingly irrelevant to modern life." — *John Hick*

Chapter 1

FACING REALITIES

"We only believe it to be true if we feel it to be true."
— *Andrew Motion*

The Emperor, who was a very vain man, had a suit of new clothes. They had been made for him by two weavers who told him the clothes were not only of the most wonderful colours and patterns, but would be invisible to anyone who was not fit for the office they held, or who was a fool. The Emperor thought that was a great idea: he would be able to find out which people he should dismiss, and sort the wise from the fools. He had wanted to see the cloth in the making, but was just a little nervous that he himself might see nothing at all on the loom, so he sent first one, then another, of his ministers. Each was appalled when he saw nothing there, but realised he could not say so. Each claimed the cloth to be beautiful, charming. When finally the Emperor was dressed in his new clothes, including an invisible train, all his courtiers exclaimed over the design and the colours. Out into the streets he went, under a gorgeous canopy, and all the people said how beautiful the Emperor's new clothes were. They did not want to be thought fools, or unfit for their posts.

Until: "But he has got nothing on," a small child said.

"Oh, listen, a child says he has nothing on."

And at last: "But he has nothing on," all the people cried.

Hans Christian Andersen's story ends: "The Emperor writhed, for he knew it was true, but he thought 'the procession must go on now', so he held himself stiffer than ever, and the chamber-lains held up the invisible train."[1]

The story of the Emperor's new clothes throws an uncomfortable light on the state of belief in the Christian Church at this time. The ways that were found, 2,000 years ago, to express how belief in God had been opened up by the existence of Jesus of Nazareth, were the ways of that time. They were the products of first-century thinking, coloured by first-century ideas about the world. Many of them are still valid today. But many are not. And, like the courtiers and the subjects of the Emperor, we do not like to say so; in some cases we do not even like to allow ourselves to think so.

Yet problems with specific items of belief will not go away. Someone will say on air or in the press that they do not believe that Jesus was born of a virgin woman, for example, or they don't think that it is right to describe a human being as God, and a great commotion of outrage is unleashed, along with a few small voices of support. The outrage is understandable: it is a fearful thing to feel that your foundations are being swept away from underneath you. The insecurity that these foundation-shakings engender, whether known consciously or unconsciously, does not make a healthy Church.

There are many reasons why, in these early years of the new millennium, we are increasingly noticing that the Church is shrinking. Some deny this, saying that on the contrary many sectors are growing amazingly. But in most examples that are given, it turns out that the churches which are growing are those tending towards fundamentalism. It is moderate Christianity that is dying, because it is neither comfortingly rigid nor creatively open.

We are living at a watershed time. Falling away behind us is the institutional Church, which has become top-heavy with authority and control. This is true of all the denominations, in varying degrees. Precisely because they *are* organisations, no matter how divinely inspired, this was inevitable. "Everything begins in prayer and ends in politics," the French writer Charles Péguy said wryly. And spreading out in front of us is the future, with Christianity shrouded in mist. Is it there at all? If it is, is it recognisable?

The present turmoil in our Churches, pastoral and theological and social, is causing so much havoc that vast change is now inevitable. In the Roman Catholic Church in Ireland, clerical scandals plus a serious shortage of ordinands have led Bishop Willie Walsh to say publicly on television that "Local people have to take over ownership of the Church". The Anglican Church has by majority decision in many countries ordained women, and in some places has pioneered new forms of more local and less academic ministry. There is increasing pressure in many parts of the Catholic Church for both an end to clerical celibacy and the ordaining of women. These changes will almost certainly come about within a relatively short time, perhaps — though not necessarily — with the next pope. But for a long time they have seemed impossible, and people are leaving the Church because they have lost hope.

Yet even before the scandals broke, the Church was fading, numbers were falling. Ireland, which has been so proudly a religious country long after the rest of Europe has been "secularised", has looked for some time as if it is about to follow suit. Maybe, we think sadly, it is after all just like the rest, only slower. My belief, and the theme of this book, is that there is a major cause of this slow death of the churches that almost no-one is talking about. It is the unwillingness of all the churches, in all countries but perhaps especially now in Ireland, to look honestly and openly into what we say we believe. Disillusioned with standard theology in all the denominations, more and more people are ceasing to attend church, while others are prevented by the same from entering. And yet among these self-exiled people there is a widespread sense of loss and sadness.

It does not need to be so. The Church does not need to die if only we will start talking with each other about what we really believe. A key factor that we need to explore is that "religion" comes from two distinct parts of our brain. "We only believe it to be true if we feel it to be true," the poet Andrew Motion has said of poetry;[2] but it applies equally to religion. The right side of our brains, which deal with our senses and feelings and intuition, is where human beings initially feel, or experience, the reality of what we call God. The left side is where we analyse and rationalise that experience, naming and labelling it, codifying and cataloguing it. The left side (which also produces our organisations and structures of authority) has become all-powerful, while the right side is ignored. The consequence is that people in search of growth in spirituality are turning their backs on the very left-brained Church and looking instead to right-brain religious activities involving awe and silence, or music and dance, or awareness of our interrelatedness with the natural world. They are not interested in doctrine: they are seeking to relate to God.

Here is the good news. There are people who are going in a different direction, in small autonomous groups, reclaiming a spiritual Christianity as theirs by right. They are if necessary doing it without the authority of the hierarchical Church, though often with the blessing of local individual clergy. The religious orders tend to be supportive. There have always been such people in the history of Christianity. It is perhaps not unreasonable to suggest that there has always been a balancing between the organisational and the spiritual, and that every now and again the organisational side has become too dominant for the faithful to tolerate. Sometimes, as with the Quietists, they have been suppressed: but their influence continued. Now in our own time, with an apparently seriously ill Church, the prognosis must be that those who are finding new ways to be both Christian and spiritual will either influence the church authorities and produce change and new life — which would be the more harmonious outcome — or, if the illness really is terminal, they (and, almost inevitably, the fundamentalists) will be the Christianity of the future.

This is not a book by a theologian, or for theologians. There have been many such books, saying what this one says in far more erudite language. The trouble is, these theological works are read almost exclusively by other theologians, and what they are saying does not reach the ordinary clergy or the laity. This is a book by an ordinary parish priest with an ordinary ministerial training, who is recently retired and therefore has the time and the space to stand back from what she has been teaching and preaching for many years, to try to see the broader picture and how it appears to people without degrees in theology. It is for them that this book is written: people for whom their Christian faith is precious but non-academic, and who wish to be able to hold it with honesty and integrity.

In the pages that follow, we will be looking at Christianity's most basic beliefs, with an outline of how they have traditionally been explained, and then I will be offering some suggestions about how they might be spoken of now. It is important to state that I have no wish to unsettle those who are happy with the old ways of expressing our beliefs. If the traditional ways work for them, if those ways express the truth as they see it, that is no problem. I am writing for those to whom the old ways have become question marks that undermine their faith in God. If God is real for them but the Church's statements about God are not then we need to find new ways to talk about God. This will not affect the beingness of God, since all the words we can ever produce about God are mere reachings in the dark. Every definition of God that we produce reduces God: God is greater than all our words.

A cold rational religion is not what is being advocated in this book. It is because our ways of explaining our religion have become too rational, too head-centred, that we have begun to object to them. The mystery that clothed that religion has largely gone, and the skeletal structure that remains exposed now looks inadequate to bear its weight. If it is to be saved, then the rationality that stems from the brain will need to be balanced with the non-rational, artistic ways of expressing truth that come from the heart, ways of awe and wonder, glory and sacredness. As the numbers of people attending parish churches are dropping, we are hearing that those going to the great cathedrals are increasing. What this seems to suggest, beyond a possible desire for anonymity, is that while local churches are usually fairly prosaic buildings, the great cathedrals have an architectural, musical and liturgical splendour that provides a sense of the otherness of God, a sense of holiness, and a real experience of the divine.

One way of looking at all this is that humankind has passed from the childhood of needing to be told what to believe, and has moved into a maturity where it is not only proper but healthy that we should be able to explore what we think about God, to come to conclusions that seem right to us at the time, and to be free to declare them without fear of ostracism or charges of heresy. Ideally we should be able to do this exploring of ideas together. What is important, the centre-point of faith, is that God is a reality to us, and that there is some sort of God–us relationship. The most significant divide in religion these days is not between people with different doctrines, but between those for whom God is a real divine presence and those for whom God is primarily a set of statements.

None of this is new. In the course of this book we will be noting the writings of some of the many people who over the past 150 years have been drawing our attention to these things. I hope these reminders of other writings will be a reassurance that all of this "new" thinking has in fact been gestating for a very long time. For many decades theologians and other writers, even bishops, have been saying that definitions of faith drawn up thousands of years ago are no longer serviceable. The writer A.N. Wilson, in a book edited by the now Bishop of Wakefield, Stephen Platten, says it with perceptive sharpness:

The leadership of the churches is dishonest. There is no other word for it — unless you add cowardly. They have been theologically educated. They know that concepts such as the physical resurrection and the virgin birth are not "true" as history. But they do not dare, even at the beginning of this new millennium, to rock the boat. As a result, nearly all of us stay outside the church and watch its decline with a mixture of sorrow and *schadenfreude*. What else does an organisation expect, which so consistently refuses to be intellectually serious?[3]

Wilson is now an agnostic, but sometimes admits to a sense of loss. He is typical of many intellectuals who felt they could not in honesty stay in the Church. It is sad that nearly thirty years ago, the Irish bishop Richard Hanson was saying a very similar thing:

Drastic re-examinations are not usually popular with the clergy or the faithful of any denomination. But unless we are content that the gulf between the experts and theologians on the one hand, and the people in pew and pulpit on the other — already dangerously wide — is to become wider and wider, such a re-examination is forced upon us. This is not a question of abandoning orthodoxy. Orthodoxy can never be defended by a blind adherence to conservative views anyway. It is a matter of re-interpreting and reassessing the Christian faith in the light of the Bible, and especially of the New Testament . . . The abyss which yawns today between the experts on the one hand and the faithful on the other is dangerous, and not enough efforts are being made to bridge it.[4]

The Benedictine nun, Joan Chittister, talks about it from an autobiographical angle:

I learned to recite the catechism and keep [the] problems to myself. I learned that the silencing of thought was far too often what adults called "faith". And I learned years later

that it is just such "faith" which, in the end, stands to stamp
out faith completely.[5]

Perhaps surprisingly, it is not predominantly the young who are
now taking the lead in saying that things need to change. Don
Cupitt says, "I bump into the same little group of peripatetic radical theologians across the English-speaking world. We are all retired, and the ones who are drawing the biggest crowds are the
bishops."[6] He attributes this to audiences understanding the con-
flict between institutional role and personal integrity, but there is
a more obvious reading. If bishops can doubt traditional teachings, then one's own doubts are less threatening, more acceptable.

I believe there is a Christianity of the future to which the exiles
will be able to return with joy. It will take courage to let it come
into being. Currently there are attempts by people with a specific
set of beliefs to hijack the word "Christian" for themselves alone,
but this must surely be resisted. The name can be claimed by any
who wish to follow the teachings of Jesus Christ or choose him as
their spiritual guide, without having to pass before an Inquisition.
There is always a tension in religion between laxity and authoritarianism. But the Christian Church, whether out of hierarchical
fear, or misguided zeal, has tried to tighten the screws of authoritarianism just at a time when in all other social and cultural areas
of our lives we are growing out of it. Hopefully our leaders, and
we ourselves, will learn to relax. Only when we can allow God to
be God will our tired old religion throw off its shackles and grow
wings. Only when we can speak of the wonderful, amazing Jesus
truthfully will his teachings come alive in us, his spirit grow in us,
and light up the world again.

In the following chapter, we will be looking at why it is that we
have doctrine, how it helps some people and should therefore not
be discarded; but how it is also, for many others now, a hindrance to
faith; and how for a hundred and fifty years or more, theologians,

clergy and others have been warning that we need to find new ways of expressing the basics of it. In Chapter Three, we look at the difference between left-brain and right-brain religion: that is, between the way we "grasp" God with the rational side of our brain and with the intuitive side. Chapter Four takes up some of our most basic doctrines and considers if there are ways that they might be newly expressed, ways that stay true to the spirit of their original formulation but also allow them be accepted by people who are aware that we no longer think in the way people thought one thousand or two thousand years ago. Chapter Five tries to work out new ways of looking with honesty and integrity at the Bible, sacraments, worship and prayer; while Chapter Six does the same for issues of lifestyle, relationships, and ethics or moral values. Chapter Seven pleads for a new openness in our churches: we need to be able to talk about these things, and we need to allow people hold varying views on doctrinal matters, without feeling that our individual faith or the Church as a whole are threatened. Chapter Eight shows that many Christians are already quietly thinking in these "new" ways that are not actually new at all, and seeks to identify the seeds of the new Church that are already being sown.

A word about the churches in Ireland: throughout this book I will be using the words "Catholic" and "Protestant" in the way in which they are commonly used here. That is to say, the word "Catholic" meaning the Roman Catholic Church, and the word "Protestant" covering the Church of Ireland (Anglican), Presbyterian, Methodist and any of the other churches which in other places are known as the Free Churches and the Reformed Churches. The Church of Ireland, of which I am a member, is in an odd position in this country. As part of the worldwide Anglican Communion it considers itself for historic and theological reasons to be both Catholic and Reformed — as indeed its church notice boards occasionally proclaim. Therefore, if pressed, many of its members would prefer to say there are not two but three main bodies of Christians in Ireland: Catholics, Anglicans, and Protestants. To further complicate the matter, in many parts of the world, the Anglican Church is called the Episcopal Church. On the other hand, quite a lot of Church of Ireland people barely recognise the words "Anglican" or "Episcopal", and most Catholics would be puzzled by them. In countries where the Anglican Church is larger, and therefore more varied, one strand of it is in many ways close to Catholicism and calls itself "Anglo-Catholic". It is for this reason that such Anglicans nearly always call Catholics "Roman Catholics": a reminder that Anglicans and Catholics are two different parts of the "one, holy, catholic Church", as all our Creeds describe it.

And, since this is a book attempting to speak about the Christian Church as a whole, not just one denomination or church, a word about myself. I was brought up as a Catholic, having an Irish Catholic mother and a Welsh Presbyterian/Methodist father. I was a very devout child, but in my late teens became an intellectual rebel and left the Church. Ten years later, in England, I rediscovered Christianity with great joy. My nearest church was Anglican. Community was important to me, and it seemed right to worship with the people I met at the school gates and in the village shop, rather than go to the unknown Catholic Church, several miles away. I became active in my local church, and years later was ordained priest in the Church of England, working as Curate and then Vicar in two parishes in Norwich. In 1996 I was appointed Rector of a parish in County Cork, and my husband and I moved to Ireland, where we remain following my retirement in 2001. Through all this I retain a real, though often grieving, affection for the Catholic Church and a real, though often grieving, affection for the Church-of-England, Church-of-Ireland, Anglican Church.

Notes

[1] Hans Christian Andersen, *Andersen's Fairy Tales* (Wordsworth Children's Classics, 1993).

[2] Andrew Motion, in interview, "Laureate and Hardy" (*Observer*, 15 September 2002).

[3] A.N. Wilson, "Christianity and Modernity", in *Ink and Spirit: Literature and Spirituality*, edited by Stephen Platten (Canterbury Press, 2000).

[4] R.P.C. Hanson, "The Dangerous Gulf between Pulpit and Pew", in *The Times*, 11 May 1974.

[5] Joan Chittister, OSB, *In Search of Belief* (Redemptorist Press, 1999).

[6] Don Cupitt, "Elderly bishops are revolting", in *The Guardian*, 5 August 2002.

Chapter 2

NEW WAYS TO EXPRESS OLD TRUTHS

"The truths preserved in our sacred doctrine can retain the
same substance under different forms of expression"
— *Pope John XXIII*

In P.D. James's novel *Death in Holy Orders*,[1] there is a bluff busi-nessman, Sir Alred, who unexpectedly asks Inspector Dalgliesh about the Nicene Creed. This is the statement of Christian belief that is used to this day in all our churches during the Eucharist (which is also known as the Mass, the Lord's Supper, Holy Communion, etc). Older forms differ slightly between Catholic and Protestant versions: here is the modern version, which is common to both.

> We believe in one God,
>> the Father, the Almighty,
>> maker of heaven and earth,
>> of all that is, seen and unseen.
>
> We believe in one Lord, Jesus Christ,
>> the only Son of God,
>> eternally begotten of the Father,
>> God from God, Light from Light,
>> true God from true God,
>> begotten, not made,
>> of one Being with the Father.
>> through him all things were made.
>> For us [men], and for our salvation

he came down from heaven:
by the power of the Holy Spirit
he became incarnate from the Virgin Mary,
and was made man.
For our sake he was crucified under Pontius Pilate:
he suffered death and was buried.
On the third day he rose again
in accordance with the Scriptures;
he ascended into heaven,
and is seated at the right hand of the Father.
He will come again in glory to judge the living and the dead,
and his kingdom will have no end.

We believe in the Holy Spirit, the Lord, the giver of life,
who proceeds from the Father and the Son.
With the Father and the Son he is worshipped and glorified.
He has spoken through the Prophets.
We believe in one holy catholic and apostolic Church.
We acknowledge one baptism for the forgiveness of sins.
We look for the resurrection of the dead,
and the life of the world to come. Amen.

We know just the sort of Christian Sir Alred is: a few paragraphs earlier he has said that he "shows his face in church from time to time". Dalgliesh, who fortunately just happens to be a vicar's son, searches his memory and tells him the Creed was formulated by the Council of Nicaea in 325 AD, and that the Emperor Constantine had called the Council "to settle the belief of the Church and to deal with the Arian heresy". To which Sir Alred retorts:

> Why doesn't the Church bring it up to date? We don't look
> to the fourth century for our understanding of medicine or
> science or the nature of the universe. I don't look to the
> fourth century when I run my companies. Why look to 325
> for our understanding of God?

Dalgliesh replies that "the Church probably takes the view that the bishops at Nicaea were divinely inspired". Sir Alred says:

It was a council of men, wasn't it? Powerful men. They
brought to it their private agendas, their prejudices, their
rivalries. Essentially it was about power, who gets it, who
yields it. You've sat on enough committees, you know how
they work. Ever known one that was divinely inspired?

Asked if he was thinking of writing to the Archbishop, or the
Pope, Sir Alred replies that he is too busy.

Anyway it's a bit outside my province. Still, it's interesting.
You'd think that it would have occurred to them.

You'd think that it would have occurred to them. Indeed. The
question of whether we can go on expressing our ideas about God
in fourth-century terms is one that we really do have to face up to
now if the Church is not to slide into a morass of well-meaning
dishonesty.

Sunday by Sunday, countless Christians, reciting the Creeds in
church, have the experience of metaphorically crossing their fingers behind their backs when they say some particular set of
words. This brings a sense of dishonesty, of integrity apparently
having to be set aside for the greater good. It does no good for the
health of the Church. We continue as uneasy Christians, unwilling
to face into questions of doctrine, seeing the decline brought about
by all this unhealthiness, but hoping the Church will at least last
our own lifetime.

Meanwhile, as Don Cupitt has observed:

Where people attempt to hold religious meanings un-
changed, their notion of faith becomes increasingly irra-
tional and authoritarian.[2]

So that if this pattern continues, Christianity will be represented
almost entirely by those who believe that the whole of the Bible is
divinely inspired and cannot be wrong; and who therefore reject
twenty-first-century ideas regarding, among other things, science,

sexuality and theology. For one of the world's great religions to end in such a narrow corner would be tragic.

For moderate Christianity to live, changes must happen. Some are already happening under the pressure of events — structural, institutional changes. But in the long term, the most serious threat to the survival of moderate Christianity lies in the matter of what we believe — the way we express our faith. Increasingly, intelligent and educated people are letting go their connection with Christianity because they cannot in good conscience say or sing the words that are expected of them in church. Others, both clergy and lay people, who stay in the Church feel uneasy or guilty about the things to which they are apparently assenting. In this state, their faith is withering even while they are ostensibly holding on to it. All of this is unacknowledged. The clergy on the whole do not preach the new thinking, which most of them will have encountered in their theological training, for fear of disturbing the faith of their congregations. The people in the pews do not tell their clergy what they really believe or do not believe, for fear of shocking them. And so a situation of the Emperor's New Clothes exists, with countless numbers saying they "see" what in truth they know is not there. Meanwhile, Christianity is not attractive to outsiders because it is clearly based on what are to them unbelievable concepts. Gradually the Church is dividing into one of authority and fundamentalist certitude, that is growing (along with fundamentalism in other world faiths), and another of individual integrity, which is shrinking.

There are voices in the wilderness, proclaiming the need to re-affirm the basic truths of Christianity by letting go the unnecessary and building on the good. These voices go back a surprisingly long way, at least into the nineteenth century. Biblical scholarship brought a flurry of them early in the twentieth century. Some of these prophets were excoriated, some lost their jobs or potential promotion because of what they were saying. But by the second half of the twentieth century, even bishops were picking up the new thinking of the theologians and were themselves publishing similar views. Yet it was in the opening years of this twenty-first century that Andrew Furlong, an Anglican priest in the Church of Ireland, was threatened with a heresy trial for making public such views — a situation only resolved by his resigning his post.[3] Such enforced lack of integrity and truthfulness can only lead to the demise of the Church.

The picture that is being built up is one of a widespread change in doctrinal thinking that is not on the whole being acknowledged. Sometimes surveys, although surprisingly little reported in the secular press, show how belief is changing. Early in 2002, the Anglican *Church Times* published the results of a survey of 8,000 readers, which showed that in the Church of England only 62 per cent of people (laity and clergy combined) believe that Jesus was born of a virgin, only 79 per cent believe in the bodily resurrection of Jesus, and a mere 12 per cent believe that "the Bible is without any errors". Six months later, as the result of another and very professional survey, the organisation Cost of Conscience claimed that out of 1,700 Anglican clergy in England only 46 per cent of them believe that Jesus is the unique means of salvation; only 61 per cent believe in the bodily resurrection of Jesus, and only 46 per cent believe in the virgin birth.

If the Church is to survive, then, the question of what as Christians we believe will have to be brought out into the open. We need to talk about doctrine itself: what is the purpose of it, where did it all come from, why is some of it so detailed? Does doctrine still serve its original purpose, or is it that it helps some people and hinders far more? Is it actually bringing the Church down? "'Orthodox' statements tell you more about who's in charge than what is true," John Pridmore has said.[4]

Most importantly, can we find new ways of expressing our basic beliefs, without invalidating the old ways that still feed the faith of many? There are plenty of people in the Church for whom the old ways of talking about God and about Jesus are perfectly valid. I remember with gratitude the times in my life when they have been valid for me and the source of great joy. I remember with thankfulness the books and places and experiences from which I learnt those ways, and the people who taught me. I see no reason why such ways should be abandoned *as long as they are helpful.* The reality is that there are many ways of expressing truth: but until now only the old ways have been officially permitted. It is time for new thinking to be allowed and accepted.

This is a matter for all our Churches. In a book written for Roman Catholic students, Clare Richards says:

> Theologians need to examine the past. They have to under-stand what the words used then meant in that time, and within that culture. They may then use new, contemporary terminology, or put new interpretations on to old ideas. Not all Catholics are aware of this need of research and re-interpretation, in spite of occasional recommendations from Rome for this work to continue. It should be realised that the great theologians of the past (Anselm, Thomas Aquinas, Teilhard de Chardin, for example), had their critics too. Pope John XXIII wrote in 1962: "The substance of faith is one thing; the way it is presented is another. For the truths preserved in our sacred doctrine can retain the same sub-stance under different forms of expression." *(Documents of Vatican II)* [5]

It is not that the old definitions are no longer true, but that they were originally set out in such language because it was the only way then that people could express the inexpressible; and now we need to restate them because otherwise we tend to take them too literally. Religion is not science. It is not a series of facts. It cannot therefore be written down as statements of facts, beyond the most basic ones. It is closer to art, or music, or poetry, where something is expressed obliquely and the truth is glimpsed through that obliqueness. John Habgood, former Archbishop of York, and a scientist by training, was getting at this when he wrote: "All truth depends on metaphor, because only through metaphor is it possible to imagine the unimaginable."[6]

Two thousand years after people made those first attempts, we are aware in increasing numbers that the old ways no longer work for us. We are very different people from them. We need to feel our way through to what it was they were trying to say then about God; and particularly about one man called Jesus in whom people had seen the likeness of God, a person whose spirit still influenced them after his death.

Tertullian (c.160–220 AD) wrote: "I believe because it is impossible . . ." He was talking about the birth of Christ. *"Credo quia impossibile"*. Or, *"Certum est quia impossibile est"*: "It is certain because it is impossible." Those few words show us how far away we are from the thinking of the early Church. They are words of paradox, a way of deliberately confounding reason so as to emphasise the nature of God as being beyond our thinking. Poets, artists, mystics and contemplatives still understand paradox, and value it. In artistic-contemplative mode, we may value many of the words of our liturgies that we know are outside rational thinking. But to most down-to-earth people of today "I believe because it is impossible" is quite simply nonsense. And those are the people that the Church is either losing, or failing to attract.

We are asking them, if they want to be part of our religious communities, to assent for example to the idea that a baby boy could be born to a woman who has not had sex with anyone; that a man who had been dead three days could get up and walk about again; and that all this and more is possible because this man, this human being, was "of the same substance" as the indefinable being/spirit/force that we call God. In rational terms it is both as meaningful and as meaningless as to say that the person I love is the sun and the moon to me. I might say that, in an emotional moment, but I would not hold out for its being literally true. Whereas Christians are being asked to state that poetic-paradox statements about God are literally true.

At this point it is important to say that what this book is *not* trying to do is to say that this or that doctrine or belief is simply "not true". We will need to look at the whole matter of what Truth is: but it is enough to say again here that religion is not science. The questions "True or False?", "Yes or No?" cannot be applied to religion (although sadly they often are) since faith is not subject to proof. If something is true for you, if this or that is the way God becomes accessible to you, then that for you *is* truth. What was truth for me in my twenties differs quite a lot from the perceptions of truth I attained in my forties: each was true in its own time. As our experience of God grows and changes we will need different ways of expressing the reality of God as it is to us. These different ways do not affect the beingness of God, since God is in any case far greater than anything we can produce in words or ideas.

But unfortunately the Christian Church, like any large organisation that wants to keep a hold on its members, has tried in varying degrees to control what we say and think. Going back to the Nicene Creed, it is important to notice that it was drawn up at a time when schisms were occurring in the Church. They were occurring because so many different intellectual ways of talking about Jesus were being put about, particularly Arianism. Arianism said, to put it in a nutshell, that God was unchangeable, but that in the *Logos* incarnate (the Word of God made human), as Jesus, he was subject to change. That was declared a heresy, and the Nicene creed was the answer to it. Around 380 AD there is the first mention of the Apostles' Creed, along with the legend that it had been formulated by the twelve Apostles themselves. It reached its final form in about the eighth century, and is regularly used at baptisms and in daily services. At around 400 AD, another creed, the Athanasian, was drawn up.

> ... We worship one God in Trinity, and Trinity in Unity;
> Neither confounding the Persons: nor dividing the Substance.
> For there is one Person of the Father, another of the Son: and another of the Holy Ghost.
> But the Godhead of the Father, of the Son, and of the Holy Ghost, is all one: the Glory equal, the Majesty co-eternal.
> Such as the Father is, such is the Son: and such is the Holy Ghost.
> The Father uncreate, the Son uncreate: and the Holy Ghost uncreate.
> The Father incomprehensible, the Son incomprehensible: and the Holy Ghost incomprehensible.

That came out of a time when more "heresies" apparently needed repressing, heresies such as Apollinarianism (the view that in Christ there was a human body and a human soul but that the mind was God's). People tend to think of the creeds as complete outlines of Christian belief and therefore as a test of orthodoxy, whereas in fact they were simply rebuttals of particular ideas, especially ideas about Jesus, at particular times in history.

Many of our other doctrines — about the death of Jesus and what it achieved, about sin and heaven and hell, about the place of Mary the mother of Jesus, about human relationships, about worship, and sacraments, and the "kingdom" of God and, through all of these, about our relationship with God — have come from our understanding of the Scriptures and from the traditions of the Church. But the science of the methods of interpreting Scripture (known as hermeneutics) has changed through the centuries. Even tradition is not set in concrete but evolves, adding here and casting off there. So our thinking on all of those subjects has altered. Sometimes the alterations have been so gradual that a specific generation would hardly have noticed them. But at other times, such as the Reformation, there have been huge doctrinal upheavals, and separations between believers. Without a doubt such abrupt upheavals will have been accompanied by great distress for some. What humans believe about God touches many bases of emotional security and stability. In some forms of Christianity these bases have often been built precisely and essentially on the "impossibility" of such beliefs. The fact that others also believe these "impossible" things can be a strong factor in community-building. But to then have the foundations pulled away from underfoot by sudden change can be devastating. Part of the shock may be a feeling of having been duped or betrayed by what then seems the calculating dishonesty of those others. And yet the changes, sudden or gradual, have continued. And will continue; and need to continue.

A book called *Das Leben Jesu — The Life of Jesus —* by D.F. Strauss is generally seen as the beginning of the new way of thinking about Christianity. It was published in Germany in 1835–6, nearly 170 years ago. Putting the view that the supernatural elements in the Gospels were part of an unintentionally created legend that had grown up in the years between the death of Jesus and the writing of the Gospels, it caused a sensation and Strauss was dismissed from his post as lecturer at Tübingen University. Some twenty years later, the book was published in London, translated into English by the novelist George Eliot, the author of *Mill on the Floss, Middlemarch*, etc. Although Eliot had long ago concluded that Jesus was a gifted teacher but not the Son of God, she was oppressed by Strauss's blunt iconoclasm. Her biographer says:

> All her life she had read the Bible not simply as the revelation of God, but as the metaphorical language of her own experience. . . . Her disillusionment with *Das Leben Jesu* became particularly acute at the beginning of 1846, when she tackled the detailed analysis of the crucifixion and resurrection. . . . To pull herself through this Slough of Despond she placed a cast of the Risen Christ . . . in a prominent place by her desk. This was her way of reasserting the mystery and hopeful joy of the New Testament narratives

which continued to sustain her long after she had given up
orthodox Christianity.[7]

She is a reminder to us that changing our view of the literal truth of
the Bible stories need not deprive us of their wonder and joy. In
1910, *The Quest of the Historical Jesus*, the translation of a book by
another German, Albert Schweitzer, made more waves. Schweitzer,
primarily a doctor and musician, had set out to find the "historical"
Jesus so as to enlarge his reality, but ended by discovering a man
who was only of his own time. The Jesus who "founded the Kingdom of Heaven upon earth and died to give His work its final con-
secration" was an ecclesiastical construction.[8]

Many other such books followed. Some were written by
clergy, but mostly they came from theologians, people whose
whole academic lives were spent in the search for ways to talk
about God, and their books do not generally reach a non-
academic public. An exception would be the writings of the German pastor Dietrich Bonhoeffer, who was hanged by the SS during World War II. A Lutheran, he had in the pre-war years
discovered with joy first Roman Catholic liturgy and then Anglican spirituality. His *Letters and Papers from Prison*, first published
posthumously in English in 1953, made an impact on many thinking Christians and has become a spiritual classic. He talked about
"religionless Christianity": the expression was often misunder-
stood, but was a recognition that humanity had reached a stage
where it felt no need of "religion" or of personal salvation, and
that God was calling us to a new form of Christianity.

> The time when people could be told everything by means
> of words, whether theological or pious, is over . . . and so is
> the time of inwardness and conscience — and that means
> the time of religion in general. . . . What do a Church, a
> community, a sermon, a liturgy, a Christian life mean in a
> religionless world? . . . In what way are we "religionless-
> secular" Christians, in what way are we — those who are
> called forth — not regarding ourselves from a religious

point of view as specially favoured, but rather as belonging wholly to the world? In that case Christ is no longer an object of religion, but something quite different, really the Lord of the world.[9]

"Christ is no longer an object of religion." Important words. And that was published exactly fifty years ago.

In 1961, attention was drawn to one of the core documents of the Anglican Church, the Thirty-Nine Articles, by W.R. Matthews, who was at that time Dean of St Paul's, London. The Articles have long been a source of unease or even rejection by some Anglicans, not least because of their unpleasant sixteenth-century mindset regarding the Roman Catholic Church (for example, they describe Masses as "blasphemous fables and dangerous deceits"). In parts of the Anglican Communion, clergy no longer have to swear assent to the Articles, but in Ireland this is still required. At a time when 61 per cent of Anglican clergy in England do not believe in the physical resurrection of Jesus,[10] it is odd that in other countries such as Ireland they are still assenting without objection to, for example, Article 4 which states that the flesh and bones of Jesus are in heaven. Back then in 1961 the Dean wrote:

> The fundamental complaint that I have to make is that the Articles do not represent the present mind of the [Anglican] Church. They have a value as representing what was the mind of the Church at the Reformation and after, but they have now merely historical interest. The mind of the Church has moved on, as I believe, under the guidance of the Holy Spirit. . . . How many of us, I wonder, would be prepared to defend in all details the language of the Articles on the Resurrection and Ascension, with the crass literalism of the assertion that the bones of the Lord Jesus are in heaven? . . . It is mistaken to minimise the influence of the Articles on the development of the drift away from the Church. That drift began long ago, and the neglect of our nineteenth century forefathers to repair the defects in our statement of doctrine has left a troublesome legacy to us . . . Why did so many of

the leading writers of that period who were by no means ir-
religious stand aloof from, or indignantly renounce, Christianity? . . . At least part of the answer would be that they
assumed, as they had good reason to do, that the teaching of
the Articles was that of the Christian Church, and found it
repugnant to their reason and conscience. We have to do the
work now which our predecessors shirked.[11]

But that was published over forty years ago, and the Articles are
still in place. More recently, Victor Griffin, the former Dean of St
Patrick's Cathedral in Dublin, has called for all the churches to remove from their confessional statements "that which is negative
and offensive to fellow Christians", including the Thirty-Nine Articles, but also the Presbyterian Westminster Confession, which
refers to the Pope as the anti-Christ, and Pope Leo XIII's statement
that Anglican Holy Orders are "absolutely null and utterly void".[12]

In 1963, John A.T. Robinson, then Bishop of Woolwich in England, caused another storm, and a new breaking open of old
thinking, with his book *Honest to God*. Suddenly, theology was
popular with ordinary people: they talked about the book at par-
ties and coffee mornings, in offices and on buses. It was basically
saying at a popular level what various theologians, particularly
Paul Tillich and Dietrich Bonhoeffer, had been saying more aca-
demically in the first half of the twentieth century. It was rejecting
as unhelpful the notion of God as a majestic and powerful personal being, and the concept of Jesus as God "visiting" the earth
in the person of "his Son".

However guardedly it may be stated, the traditional view
leaves the impression that God took a space-trip and arrived
on this planet in the form of a man. Jesus was not really one
of us; but through the miracle of the Virgin Birth he con-
trived to be born so as to appear one of us. Really he came
from outside. I am aware that this is a parody, but I think it
is perilously near the truth of what most people — and I
would include myself — have been brought up to believe at

Christmas time. Indeed, the very word "incarnation" (which, of course, is not a Biblical term) almost inevitably suggests it. It conjures up the idea of a divine substance being plunged in flesh and coated with it like chocolate or silver plating. And if that is a crude picture, substitute for it that of the Christmas collect, which speaks of the Son of God "taking our nature upon him", or that of Wesley's Christmas hymn, with its "veiled in flesh the Godhead see".

The bishop was not seeking to abolish the Christmas story. It is indeed a myth, he says, but myth is not only legitimate but also important. Myth indicates the significance and "divine depth" of events.

We shall be grievously impoverished if our ears cannot tune to the angels' song or our eyes are blind to the wise men's star. But we must be able to read the nativity story without assuming that its truth depends on there being a literal interruption of the natural by the supernatural, that Jesus can only be Emmanuel — God with us — if, as it were, he came through from another world. For, as supernaturalism becomes less and less credible, to tie the action of God to such a way of thinking is to banish it for increasing numbers into the preserve of the pagan myths and thereby to sever it from any real connection with history.[13]

That book was published forty years ago. It is hard to credit that what was said by a bishop then is subjected to the charge of heresy when it is said by clergy now.

Another key book was *The Myth of God Incarnate*, a set of essays by various Anglican clergy and theologians, edited by John Hick and published in 1977. The opening essay, by Maurice Wiles, is titled "Christianity without Incarnation?", and the other essays develop that theme. The epilogue, by Dennis Nineham, asks three concluding questions. The first is whether it is "any longer worthwhile to attempt to trace the Christian's ever-changing understanding of his relationship with God directly back to some identifiable element in the life, character and activity of Jesus of Nazareth?" The second is whether, if such an attempt is made, it will "lead inevitably to a degree of sophistication which is unintelligible to the majority of Christians". The third is whether it is necessary to believe in Jesus beyond seeing him as the man through whom God brought people into so rich a relationship with himself as to be the salvation of a large part of humanity. The book was a set course book in my own theological training in the early 1980s. Some students were disturbed by it, and one or two rejected it, but most took it in their stride.

All of these have been Anglican or Protestant writers. In the Roman Catholic Church, during this period, a parallel process has been going on, but with the difference that the impetus for change came initially from the top of the hierarchy. The Second Vatican Council, meeting in the early 1960s under Pope John XXIII and then Pope Paul VI, made enormous changes at root level to the Church, opening huge doors and letting in light and air. Distressing to a minority, it was to the majority a great release into healthy new creativity. At about the same time, Liberation Theology developed, offering Christianity as a revolutionary force, with Jesus as an alternative to Karl Marx. This was "the doctrine of social struggle", which became especially strong in South America.[14] But in the decades that followed, the doors were to some extent pulled closed again. Attempts were made to silence writers like Hans Küng, Leonardo Boff, Gustavo Gutiérrez, Tissa Balasuriya, Lavinia Byrne and others. Radical thinking went largely underground.

Why do we have doctrines at all? And where have we got them from? It seems evident that they have come about in two or three different ways.

One — dating back to the earliest of Christian writings, the epistles and gospels — would be the desire to put a great experience into words so that it can be conveyed to others.

The second, from a time when the Church was beginning to grow beyond easy control by its leaders, would be from a sense that some people were saying the wrong things, giving the wrong impressions, spreading the wrong message. The Church therefore wanted to create definitions that would decide who was in, and who was out, of this swelling organisation. Most organisations that have moved from small beginnings into something big will recognise this stage of development.

A third, coming from scholars and theologians, would be their desire to see the truths that they have pursued and studied more widely known. For example:

- Thomas Aquinas in the thirteenth century used the term "articles of faith" to describe revealed doctrine, primarily "that God exists and that he has providence over man's salvation". Faith in the providence of God, he says, includes all the things that God arranges for our redemption, and faith in that redemption "*implies* Christ's Incarnation and Passion and all related matters" (my italics). This was intended to establish the conclusions of theology in a scientific manner, though to modern ears it seems not only not scientific but not even logical.

- In 1571, the newly formed Anglican Church put together Thirty-Nine Articles of faith, which in 1961 the Dean of St Paul's described as "the only authoritative statement of the distinctive doctrines of our Church" (even though, as we saw earlier, he said it was time for them and their out-of-date theology to go).[15]

- In the twentieth century, Vatican II declared the basic articles of faith to be the doctrines of the Trinity, the Incarnation, and human redemption.

- In between these large statements, there have been smaller, but often very significant, summaries of belief. An example would be the Niagara Fundamentals, drawn up nearly a century ago by Protestant conservatives. Their list consisted of: the inerrancy of the Bible, the creation of the world in seven

days, the incarnation of God in Christ, substitutionary atonement (the idea that Jesus was crucified in place of past and future sinners), and the bodily resurrection of Jesus.

For many Christians, Catechisms have been the most direct way
into Christian doctrine. They have existed since the Middle Ages,
some being the work of one author, others of whole committees.
The Reformation brought a great rush of new catechisms, Lutheran and Calvinist, Anglican and Presbyterian. Nearly all included one of the Creeds, the Lord's Prayer and the Ten
Commandments, with explanations. The Roman Catholic Church
then followed, with similar contents and additions such as the
Hail Mary and the Commandments of the Church. Different countries, even different dioceses, had their own versions: the "Penny
Catechism" came out in England in 1898. A hugely expanded
universal Catechism came from the Vatican in 1994.

Although many in the churches like to think that doctrine is
firm and immoveable, in reality the beliefs of most of us are
changing, although so gradually as to be almost imperceptible at
any one point. Ideas of heaven and hell are a good example of
this. When did we stop thinking that these were actual places, one
above the world and one below? Was it an individual thing, happening when we reached a certain level of maturity or education?
Or a case of social conditioning, all or most of us finally influenced by the mass communication of what the serious thinkers
were saying? Or was it a matter of morphic resonance — something in the universal consciousness that suddenly found a place
in all our minds? Whatever about that, few people now would
claim to hold those old flat-earth ideas. Yet officially some parts of
the Church still hold them. The scientist Richard Dawkins has
written recently:

> Nowadays, we are told, religion has moved on. Heaven is
> not a physical place, and God does not have a physical
> body where a beard might sit. Well, yes, admirable . . . But

the doctrine of the Assumption was defined as an Article of Faith by Pope Pius XII as recently as November 1st, 1950, and is binding on all Catholics. It clearly states that the *body* of Mary was taken into Heaven and reunited with her soul. What can that mean, if not that Heaven is a physical place, physical enough to contain bodies?[16]

Behind every doctrinal pronouncement lies a truth waiting to say something real. The Catholic priest Adrian B. Smith says:

Doctrines are always partial expressions of the Truth. . . . To retain old formularies as if they had an eternal value and not constantly to be re-formulating them in the light of present-day knowledge, can lead to our being unfaithful to the original revelation.[17]

And the Anglican theologian Maurice Wiles writes:

It is worthwhile [for the doctrinal critic who is also a Christian] to worry away at what lies at the heart of, underneath, or at the back of, traditional doctrinal statements; in their old form they may no longer make satisfactory sense for him in relation to his honest attempts to understand the world in which he lives in all its depth, but that is not the same thing as to say that he regards them as unimportant or valueless . . . Every Christian theologian must expect the charge of being unfaithful either to the historical tradition of Christian faith or to the realities of the modern world. But that is no argument against the propriety of the task.[18]

In Chapter 4 we will look at some of the basic Christian doctrines: at how they have been traditionally expressed, and at the concepts that must have lain behind those formulations. We then look at ways in which they might be newly expressed. But before that, it may be helpful to consider *how* we experience God and matters concerning God, and it is to this that we turn in Chapter 3.

Notes

[1] P.D. James, *Death in Holy Orders* (Faber and Faber, 2001).

[2] Don Cupitt, *The Sea of Faith* (BBC, 1984).

[3] Andrew Furlong, *Tried for Heresy: A 21st Century Journey of Faith* (John Hunt, 2003).

[4] In review of Richard Harries' book, *God Outside the Box*, in *Church Times*, 11 October 2002.

[5] Clare Richards, *Introducing Catholic Theology* (Kevin Mayhew, 2002).

[6] John Habgood, "Help with Saying the Unsayable" (book review), in *Church Times*, 3 January 2003.

[7] Kathryn Hughes, *George Eliot: The Last Victorian* (Fourth Estate, 1998).

[8] Albert Schweitzer, *The Quest of the Historical Jesus,* trans. W. Montgomery (A&C Black, 1954).

[9] Dietrich Bonhoeffer, *Letters and Papers from Prison* (SCM Press, 1953).

[10] *Church Times* survey, 2002.

[11] W.R. Matthews, *The Thirty-Nine Articles: A plea for a new statement of the Christian faith as understood by the Church of England* (Hodder & Stoughton, 1961).

[12] Victor Griffin, *Enough Religion to Make Us Hate* (Columba, 2002).

[13] John A.T. Robinson, *Honest to God* (SCM Press, 1963).

[14] Jean Milet, *God or Christ?* trans. John Bowden (SCM Press, 1981).

[15] W.R. Matthews, *The Thirty-Nine Articles: A plea for a new statement of the Christian faith as understood by the Church of England* (Hodder & Stoughton, 1961).

[16] Richard Dawkins, *A Devil's Chaplain* (Weidenfeld & Nicholson, 2003).

[17] Adrian B. Smith, *A New Framework for Christian Belief* (CANA, 2001).

[18] Maurice Wiles, *Working Papers in Doctrine* (SCM, 1976).

Chapter 3

LEFT-BRAIN, RIGHT-BRAIN RELIGION:
HOW WE EXPERIENCE GOD

"By love God may be caught and held: by thinking, never."
— *from* The Cloud of Unknowing, *anon., 14th century*

"The heart has its reasons, that Reason knows not of."
— *from Pascal's* Pensées

Once I prepared a graph for my parishioners, showing how many we were, with the numbers arranged in columns by age group. At the left-hand side of the paper were the under-fives, the potential future churchgoers, with a flower representing each name. The next column was the under-fifteens, and so on across the page. In each column there were a few flowers. At the far right of the page was the column for the over-sixties and that column, unlike all the others, was wonderfully full of flowers. But I asked the people to turn that end piece of the paper over, out of sight. We all stared at the small number remaining. "That's what this church will be like in twenty years' time," I said. I didn't add, "if even those few choose to stay".

The dying of the church is happening in all Christian denominations in Ireland, just as it has happened previously in other countries. Perhaps it is all the sadder here, in the country which for so long was a shining light of Christianity. Other Europeans sentimentalised, often nostalgically, about the strong and deep and natural faith of the Irish. Now it looks as if maybe, for what-

ever reasons, we were not stronger, just slower. There is not a lot
of hard evidence, but figures from the Irish Council of Churches
show that, among Roman Catholics in Ireland, weekly mass attendance fell from 91 per cent in 1974 to 57 per cent in 1999. They
also show a 24 per cent decline in membership of the Church of
Ireland from 1947 to 1996.[1] But then we have to ask, what is membership? In many Irish communities people are identified by their
past allegiance, or very often simply by the past allegiance of their
parents and grandparents. In 1998, 22 per cent of the people in
Ireland who claim to be Protestant never even went to church. A
Belfast Telegraph Millennium Generation Survey of both Protestants and Catholics in Northern Ireland found the following
church attendance pattern among people aged 25 to 45: only 33
per cent went every or almost every week; and 27 per cent never
went at all.

Sometimes we seem willing to look at this matter of falling
numbers, other times we go into denial and simply refuse to look
at the problem. For many years it was theologically fashionable for
clergy to say that numbers didn't matter, that God doesn't count
numbers. Even now, some individuals take the attitude that as
long as their church (usually their actual church building, and that
congregation's way of doing things) will be there until they die,
they have no further concern. They are not interested in why the
decline is happening, and even less interested in doing anything
that might make a change, because change itself is unwelcome.

But here is the up-side of Ireland's slowness to drop its faith in
God: that maybe we do have time to be brave and look at why the
slide into so-called secularism is happening; and a chance to re-
verse it. Not back to the grim days of Calvinistic or Ultramontan-
ist[2] rigidity but further back. We can, if we choose, reclaim that
ancient tradition of living with a sense of the daily presence of the
divine. This is something for which Ireland and Scotland and
Wales are famous. The world calls it "Celtic spirituality" and is
entranced with it. Of course there is much that is over-

romanticised and sentimentalised about "Celtic spirituality", not least the fact that, as a recent historical work reported,[3] no one thought of himself or herself as a "Celt" before about 1800. But as a rootstock for the grafting of the flower of Christianity, it has wonderful potential. A key factor is its profound sense of the presence of God in the world. As theologian John Macquarrie has written:

> It may be that the theological basis of that old spirituality, namely, an understanding of God as deeply involved in his creation, can generate a new spirituality appropriate to new social conditions.[4]

What then is killing the Church? Is it the heavy hand of ecclesiastical authority that in an educated populace no longer has power? Is it that the clerical scandals, primarily in the Catholic Church, have been the last straw, seeming to show that some of the very people who have held the reins so tightly over their parishioners were committing sins far greater than the small failures they used to hear in the confessionals week by week? Is it that the desire for tribal identification, which for so long held the Protestant denominations in rigid conformity, is less important now? Or is it that in a world suddenly full of entertainment, and very professional entertainment at that, the practice of going into a church week by week and sitting through the familiar, almost unvarying, recital of words and more words is quite simply too boring to tolerate? All of these are factors. Yet there is another factor which, if it were put right, would wipe all those others away. A factor, or rather a dual factor, which lies behind all the rest and is the key point of this book.

It is that our faith lacks the integrity of honesty. And it lacks that integrity because we have fallen into the habit of expressing what we know of God almost entirely with the rational, intellectual side of our brain, rather than letting it come out of the way we actually experience God. We, as laity and as clergy, have been mis-presenting our faith for a very long time.

One of the great mysteries of faith is the mystery of faith. What is it? Why do some people have it and others not? Often in one lifetime it can come and go, or go and come again. How much can we understand of what faith is like inside another person's head, inside their whole being? To a degree, the answer must always be "very little". In a concept known as "Nagel's bat", scientists admit that all of science is confounded by the simple awareness that it can never know what it is to be a bat. Just so, we can never entirely know what it is to be in someone else's mind. And yet we expect clergy to have some understanding of the varieties of religious experience. At the end of my Anglican theological training in the 1980s, all of us were asked if we thought anything had been lacking in the curriculum. My own response was that I would have liked more about the psychology of religious development. By that time I had been closely involved for a number of years in talking with people who practised contemplative prayer. Yet I felt I only knew enough to know how much I did *not* know about them. I also knew there was a danger of assuming that their journeys were following the same path as my journey, even though these were not a cross-section of Christians but a specific group of people, drawn as I was to one particular form of prayer. When I was ordained and began to minister in parishes I discovered among the parishioners an even wider range of religious life-stories. There were people who had been brought up in church-going families and had been regular churchgoers all their lives. There were others who after a religious upbringing had rebelled against it all — or more often against some particular aspect of religion — and had left the Church. There were a few who had rebelled and then in later life come back, either taking up where they had left off, or bringing with them a broader vision. And there were some who had no religious background at all but were on a journey of discovery into Christianity.

Those are the externals of religious observance, the easily dis-coverable facts. What goes on inside is not so easy to discern. One of the parables of Jesus concerns the sowing of seeds:

> A sower went out to sow. And as he sowed, some seeds fell on the path, and the birds came and ate them up. Other seeds fell on rocky ground, where they did not have much soil, and they sprang up quickly, since they did not have much depth of soil. But when the sun rose, they were scorched; and since they had no root, they withered away. Other seeds fell among thorns, and the thorns grew up and choked them. Other seeds fell on good soil and brought forth grain, some a hundredfold, some sixty, some thirty.[5]

For some of the parishioners, I suspected, church-going was part of a comfortable routine, one with quite real but rather short roots. For others, whether they were "new" Christians or life-long prac-titioners, the roots were incredibly deep and still spreading, draw-ing sustenance from every possible source. Some of those who had been churchgoers all their lives appeared never to have had any questions about faith or religion or God or the things of God: it is as if what they had been told in Sunday School was as unnec-essary to question as were the basics of mathematics, history and geography that they were also taught when young. But other "cradle-Christians" clearly had a lively, growing and evolving relationship with God. Many, I gradually came to realise, held unorthodox theological views and were comfortable with them but would not open them up to clergy unless they were very sure it would not distress them.

For some parishioners, I knew, the word "God" meant some sort of great and universal Being, while for others it produced a mental picture of the perfect and totally reliable human figure of Jesus. Not many people these days practise their religion because they fear eternal damnation if they do not: nevertheless, quite a few showed by what they said that they still had an image of a grim, unsmiling God, a heavy parent-figure whose demands on them could not be ignored. But just as that model has tended to fade out, so we are seeing now an increase in the number of people for whom God is to all intents and purposes a superstition: do this as it says in the Bible and you will be safe, you will be saved, you will be alright; but do that and you will be damned. Do not step on the cracks in the footpath or the bears/devil will get you. There is a relationship with God in this type of person, often a very loving one; but it is sad that the God who is loved appears so unloving.

At the other extreme from this security-seeking religion is the person with no particular religious affiliations, who nevertheless has experienced God — whether or not they would use that word. Alister Hardy and David Hay of the Religious Experience Research Unit at Oxford have done important work on this, showing that human evolution has not destroyed a widespread belief in the possibility of extra-sensory contact with "a Power which is greater than, and in part lies beyond, the individual self".[6] Their initial research prompted accounts of such contact experience from thousands of people. With the caveat that it would be a mistake to think the restructuring of Christian theology would bring all those people into our churches (David Hay has said that often people whose natural religious awareness is very rich are repelled by the institutional Church)[7], it is reasonable to think that a good percentage of them might be happy to be part of an open, non-dogmatic — and eventually non-hierarchical? — faith community.

These days many of the people who have a well-developed spirituality but have fallen away from traditional church-going, or have never seen the attraction of it, are filling up the meditation groups, whether Christian or not, the yoga and T'ai Chi groups, and even the retreat houses, especially the monastic ones where the daily office is sung. They are taking from the great religions of the world whatever will nourish and encourage their spiritual growth, while setting light to dogmatic statements. This "*à la carte*" style of religion is understandably much derided by the church hierarchies, because it draws people away from their control or influence, but it is inevitable when conditions for acceptance by the churches are being constantly tightened. The sad side of it is that for spiritual people to whom the institutional Church is more repellent than attractive, religion can become a private interest and a solo occupation.

This touches on one of the big divides in people's attitudes to religion. Even regular churchgoers can be divided into those for whom faith is a private matter and those for whom it is communal. Charismatics and contemplatives are extreme examples. In many ways poles apart, they share a common liability to have such a strong and intense personal relationship with God that the institutional Church may be written off because it does not seem to have any connection with that relationship. But even among less differentiated churchgoers, there is a divide between those who are more at home with God than with their fellow Christians. Charles Taylor claims that this tendency to privatise religion is at least partially responsible for the shrinking of the Church.[8] Although it has a long history, its increase now is clearly related to our current secular emphasis on individualism, our unwillingness to be treated as a herd, and our refusal to grant unthinking obeisance to hierarchical authority.

Since those days of my theological training, many books of the sort I was needing then have been published: books on the psychology of religious development, and on spiritual growth, and on the ways that different people experience prayer, for example. But for many, the most helpful of all developments in understanding how we relate to God has been the discovery of the functioning of the left and right sides of the human brain — the "head" side and the "heart" side, the analytical side and the intuitive side. When we sit at our desk adding up a list of sums, we are in left-brain mode. When we stop that and gaze at the beauty of the landscape outside the window, we shift into right-brain mode.

It is with the intuitive right side of the brain that people experience God, which is why so many find they are nearer to God in nature. It is with the right side of our brain that we can be emotionally overwhelmed as we look up at marvellous cathedrals or sense the presence of God as we gaze at the sky. With the right-brain we find our hearts enlarged and deepened by art and music: if we have a sense of God, it will be there in that enlargement and deepening. If Moses experienced God in the burning bush, it was with the right side of his brain. If Jacob wrestled all night with an angel — or was it God? — and Jesus heard the spirit of God calling him at his baptism, these were right-brain experiences. But when these happenings were later written down in words, they moved over into a left-side mode, where they could be rationalised, described, analysed and argued about. This left-side activity is good, and necessary; but if left-side activity is all that remains of an experience, it is potentially disastrous. It is like describing a beautiful painting, and then destroying the painting and hanging on the wall the words that describe it.

The first time I was aware of the implications of this matter of right-brain versus left brain was when I read Betty Edwards's book *Drawing on the Right Side of the Brain*,[9] which one after another of my artist friends were telling me had had a huge influence on them. As someone who has always enjoyed drawing, I discovered from the book not a new way of drawing but, to my surprise, an explanation of the way I always had drawn: a way of seeing the object — a flower or a cup or a landscape — with my senses but without rational thought. Without knowing it, and surely like many others, I had been since childhood using the right side of my brain when looking at something and conveying an image of it onto paper. No wonder I had felt that sketching was a "contemplative" pastime. It is with the right side of our brain that we hear music — unless we actually choose to be academic about it. It is with the right side of our brain that we look at art or architecture or nature — again, unless we are being deliberately academic. If we are, then it is the left side of our brain that takes over. The left side is responsible for all those rational ways of thinking, such as analysis, labelling and codifying. We can watch a singing bird on a tree and simply "be" with it, and that is right-brain activity. Or we can say to ourselves, "A red-crested warbler, I think. I wonder where its nest is?"; and that is a left-brain response. Women are sometimes accused of being all right-brain ("intuitive") and men all left-brain ("analytical"), which is of course nonsense. We are all a mixture of both, and we do need a balance of both.

It was in reading Edwards's book that I saw for the first time how unbalanced we are in our religious practices. We experience the reality of God in the right side of our brain. Yet organised religion is left-brain. In one sense, that is inevitable: organisation as such needs to be rational. But what is not inevitable, and certainly not desirable, is that our corporate communication with God should become a left-brain activity, as it largely has done. Such communication — often called "worship" — should surely bring a sense of the presence of God, or some degree of experience of God. Yet in these days, and in this country, worship is almost entirely left-brain fodder: rational and wordy, consisting of prayers, readings, creeds, homilies. With the exception of physical acts such as walking up through the church and receiving communion, or being sprinkled or immersed in water in baptism, it is all thought-material and no experience-material. In our Western culture, a service that is not a communion service has normally no experiential element at all, except for the singing of hymns, and even those are word-filled. So, paradoxically, a church service can be the most difficult place in which to pray. Too much of what we call praying is left-brain, all words and thinking, and almost no space is left for us to make contact with God. Meditation, or contemplative prayer, is that sort of space; and too many clergy and laypeople are scared stiff of it and will not let it become part of corporate worship. Even the "Let us keep silent for a moment", which is occasionally heard, rarely extends to more than thirty seconds. But in places where contemplative prayer is being discovered by small groups of people, often of mixed denominations, great steps in communal spirituality are being made.[10]

The Meaning of Worship

What then *is* worship? The origin of the word is "worthship": giving worth to God. So is it something we do for God? Or is it done in the hope that we will get something from God? Is it, more simply, a two-way communication? And is it for our benefit, or God's, or the world's? For some it is simply a duty that they do because they think God wants it of us. But if we engage in it for that reason, are we just being obedient children who, having complied with the requirements, can feel unguilty? Or is it meant to make us feel good? These would be meagre ways of looking at it. William Temple, who was Archbishop of Canterbury for just two remarkable years, 1942–44, wrote:

> Worship is to quicken the conscience to the holiness of God,
> to feed the mind with the truth of God,
> to purge the imagination with the beauty of God,
> to open the heart to the love of God,
> to devote the will to the purposes of God.

In her important book *Worship*, Evelyn Underhill says that worship is an avenue which leads us out "from inveterate self-occupation to a knowledge of God, and ultimately to that union with God which is the beatitude of the soul . . . till at last all ways and manners are swallowed up in a self-giving love".[11] This total love is the real outcome of real worship. If there is a purpose to worship it is not primarily to be nice to God or Jesus or to ourselves. According to Underhill, the purpose is the growth of love: nothing less than the transfiguration of the whole created universe.

The result of generations of word-based religious education, and worship that is word-based even when it is a sacramental form of service (such as the Eucharist, or the Mass, or Holy Com-

munion, or the Lord's Supper), is that we only know how to express our faith, our spirituality, our sense of the reality of God, in
left-brain ways. Words become all-important. More dangerous
still, words that began as poetry are required to become hard
facts. We are told that Jesus identified his body, his life, with the
ordinary — but vital — substances of bread and wine, asking his
disciples to remember him every time they take up these everyday things. But his words have become a quasi-scientific statement that these materials can, if the right words are said by the
right person, become factually the flesh and blood of Jesus.

There are many other examples of biblical words that have begun as poetry and ended as concrete. Angels filling the sky above
a straw-strewn manger become not an expression of glory and
delight but literal realities: are they male or female, we ask? What
size are they? How many can dance on the head of a pin? A virgin
giving birth to a baby who is full of God becomes not an expression of joy at the way the divine is present in all human life but a
concrete reality. How did God achieve this, we ask? What was
Joseph's part, and did Mary have other children afterwards? Such
hard-edged doctrine can become a weapon of heresy-hunters. Do
you believe in the Virgin Birth, yes or no? Jesus rose from the
dead: true or false?

Here is the crux of the matter: all credal statements about God
have come from the analytical side of the human brain, and with
that left-side they are now heard by churchgoers and church-
refusers alike. Yet the impulse to make those statements must
have come originally from right-side experiences of the reality of
God. In the Judeo-Christian scriptures, experiences too large to be
put into words were expressed in poetic words and understood
by others in the same mode: right- and left-brain combined. The
exercising of these two sides of us, right- and left-brain, or heart
and head, needs to be balanced, and sadly in our recent past the
Church has tipped almost exclusively over into left-brain, head
mode. In millions of us today, the conscious or unconscious

yearning for experiential knowledge of God is baffled and sub-
verted by being presented with left-brain answers to our questions and our longings. In past ages, an awareness of the divine
would have led us, if we were part of a Christian culture, into
feeding that awareness through participation in Christian worship, which might have included being in spaces of beautiful sim-
plicity or heart-raising splendour, our senses heightened by sight
and sound and touch and smell; hearing and singing the sort of
music that comes not just from our throat but from our blood and
bones and sinews; moving our bodies in acts of reverence which
actually generate the emotions they emulate.

If Christianity is to be saved in Ireland we need to recover this
balance of head and heart, of the rational and the intuitive. Can we
do it? If so, how do we do it? And is it in fact already happening?

The question of whether we can do it is perhaps preceded for
some by the question: Why would we want to do it? Our understanding of the great range of world faiths has broadened in past
decades to such an extent that we may well be asking why we
should be in separate little groupings at all. If a large proportion of
all human beings have a sense of the Other, the Divine, a Power or
Force at work among us, why do we need separate faiths? Why
should any of us want Christianity to survive, if we are no longer
playing the "my-religion-is-better-than-your-religion" game? I think
the answer is that, just as our bodies need feeding if they are to live,
and we are accustomed to different types of food in different cultures, so our souls need feeding and we mostly do best on whatever is culturally available to us. The centuries of Christian history
and tradition have included good and bad, but there are great
treasures there if we have the wisdom to be selective, which if we
allow them can feed us even better than they have in the past.

The primary need would seem to be to release ourselves from
the petrifying bonds of rigid expressions of religious belief. We
must be able to believe in our hearts what we say with our lips we
believe. Without this, we are lying to ourselves, crossing our fin-

gers behind our backs, while being convinced that this lying is the right thing to do because the Church has told us so; and by doing it we are binding ourselves and each other, clergy and laity, tighter and tighter into a mesh of dishonesty and dis-ease. Rigid certainties of belief, the glib and easy recourse to phrases like "the Bible says . . ." as an answer to every situation, may bring short-term security but in the long term are shackles of silent despair. The Church must lighten up, not tighten up, if it is not to be abandoned by its people. It must allow diversity of belief and diversity of practice. This does not have to be seen as a negative step but one to be taken with confidence: a step into diversity can be a step into joy and delight if we let ourselves continue to be guided by the spirit of God.

We can recover the balance if we are able to let go of the lifeless, plastic, pre-packaged formulas of belief that are head-based expressions of ancient heart-based experiences of God, and move to the fresh aliveness of how God is revealed to us in the present. This does not mean abandoning the past, but gathering up from it all that is good and life-giving, and letting go all that starves or strangles life, or is merely dead wood. Like Noah, seeing the waters rise, we must decide which things will create new life in the years ahead. There was no room for dead bodies in the ark. Though doubtless there would be memories: the past is precious to us, just as our grandparents can be precious to us; where there is wisdom and beauty and virtue we can benefit from it. But to attempt to live in the past is no more possible or desirable than to attempt to relive our grandparents' lives. This is so utterly obvious that in any other field it would be unnecessary to say it. In religion as it is being purveyed at present, it seems not to be obvious at all.

Change Can Bring New Faith

The old ways of expressing our beliefs are either being held not with their original poetic sense but as being literally true; or else they are making people increasingly aware of the need for crossed fingers until the lack of integrity becomes intolerable and they leave the Church. So it seems clear that we must find new ways of saying what we think about God, about Jesus, about the events recorded in the Bible, and about the ecclesiastical structures that have grown up in the service of defending the old certainties. We will have to search for new ways of stating the old truths. To find what they were really expressing two thousand years ago, and re-express those things in ways not untrue to our present understanding. Concepts such as the divinity of Jesus, the Fall, Atonement and Resurrection are not only driving faithful Christians away from the Church but also stopping rational and educated people from entering it. By clinging to two-thousand-year-old concepts — which we do in no other area of our lives — we deter people from becoming followers of Christ and deprive them of the joy of being part of a God-centred community.

Yet these very concepts, if we can see through the accretions that have been heaped upon them, are basically life-affirming, except for the concept of Atonement (that Jesus died to placate an angry God) which seems to have no salvageable aspect. To take the others:

- The "divinity" of Jesus is a recognition that God is present in all human life, and the man Jesus was a supreme example of that presence, so that in him people caught a glimpse of the goodness and glory of God;

- The "Fall" is a way of coming to terms with the fact that in spite of that divinity in us there is also in us a will to go against God-ness that brings us grief;

- The "Resurrection" of Jesus as the Christ ties in with one of our deepest natural human beliefs, namely that out of apparent evil and death can come new life and hope and joy. In its actual time it was a recognition that the spirit of Jesus was still with his followers after his death.

There is no need to express these ideas in ways that go against all that we know of how things are. No need to deny human reason in our religion. These things are part of life and a valid and healthful part of the way we explain the meaning of life to ourselves. It is true that in the Bible they are expressed in a poetic (right-brain) rather than a literal (left-brain) way: if we know that, we can draw nourishment and enrichment from the stories.

Increasing numbers of people are discovering that they are already thinking in these ways. The change comes gradually, subconsciously, and may cause considerable difficulty when the realisation surfaces. Yet when they find the strength to break out of the cocoon of repressed disbelief, they frequently experience faith spreading vibrant new wings.

Since there are of course many for whom the old ways of expressing the faith are perfectly satisfactory, it is vital that they should not feel that their way is no longer valid. Those of us who want the new ways to be accepted are not asking for the old ways to be thrown out. Indeed, some of the people we most respect would defend the old ways. What we want is for Christianity to become big enough to allow the old and new ways to function together, without witch hunts, without charges of "Heresy!" If God is big enough to contain Judaism and Islam and Christianity, and a lot else beside, then God can cope with our different levels of understanding. And if God can, we can surely try to do the same.

I know that some people will find this sort of thinking initially disturbing. They may never have encountered it before, or may have turned away from suspicions of it, either in themselves or coming from outside themselves. In fact, writers and theologians and clergy — even bishops — have been saying such things for a long time now, as we will be exploring more fully in the next chapter.

Notes

---

[1] Irish Council of Churches, *Statistical Snapshots on the State of Religion in Ireland* (2002).

[2] Ultramontanism is defined in the *Oxford Dictionary of the Christian Church* as "the name widely given to a tendency in the Roman Catholic Church which favours the centralisation of authority and influence in the papal Curia, as opposed to national or diocesan independence." See also *The Oxford Companion to Irish History*, ed. S.J. Connolly.

[3] A.T.Q. Stewart, *The Shape of Irish History* (Blackstaff, 2001).

[4] John Macquarrie, in *Dictionary of Christian Spirituality*.

[5] Matthew 13:28.

[6] Alister Hardy, "The Divine Flame" (The Religious Experience Research Unit, Oxford, 1966).

[7] David Hay, *Religious Experience Today* (Mowbray, 1990).

[8] Charles Taylor, *Varieties of Religion Today* (Harvard University Press, 2003).

[9] Betty Edwards, *Drawing on the Right Side of the Brain* (Souvenir Press, 1979).

[10] For example, the Julian Meetings, and the World Community of Christian Meditation.

[11] Evelyn Underhill, *Worship* (Nisbet & Co. Ltd, 1936).

Chapter 4

SOME BASIC CHRISTIAN DOCTRINES — AND NEW WAYS TO EXPRESS THEM WITH INTEGRITY

"The available language about God has been allowed to
become too narrow, stale and spiritually obsolete."
— *Don Cupitt*

One of the reasons we have reached this crisis point in our churches is that we have either shut our ears to the natural development of theology (the academic study of God) or we have had our ears shut for us. Whatever about that, the theologians have been doing their heroic best for about a hundred and fifty years to get us to move forward and keep up with that development — just as medical researchers and geologists, say, have kept us up to date with the natural development of medical knowledge and geology. For decades now, clergy in their theological training have been exposed to these writings. For many of them, they present no difficulties. The trouble is that when they go out into the world to minister to their fellow Christians they do not on the whole feel able to transmit such knowledge, partly because they have no mandate from their church authorities to do so, but also for fear of upsetting what they see as the "simple faith" of numbers of their parishioners. Thus the old, literal ways of hearing Bible readings and the statements of the creeds have continued almost unchallenged. What was, a hundred years ago, a very small gap between the theologians and the people in the pews gradually widened throughout the twentieth century. If the widening continues the two sides will soon be out of sight and sound of each other and most of the Church will have fallen into the hole. Now, at the start of the twenty-first century, is probably our last chance to get rid of the gap.

God

What can we say about God?

> "We do not know what God is." (St Thomas Aquinas)

> "If you understand, it is not God." (St Augustine)

Despite these words and others like them, a great deal has been said and written by Christians about God. Theological libraries, and even some public libraries, have shelves and shelves of books about God. Yet in the end, they could all be thrown away under the philosopher Ludwig Wittgenstein's famous dictum: "Whereof we cannot speak, thereof we must keep silence." Silence — in the sense of going beyond language into an awareness of being — is the fullest response to the presence of God, and it is in silence that we most basically experience God. The *via negativa* is an ancient method of theology which acknowledges this. Going back to the fifth century, and revived from time to time, it is a way of speaking of God while being aware that "human language is hopelessly inadequate to use of the ineffable God", and it attempts to strip away those human qualities which are inappropriate to apply to God.[1] The Eastern Orthodox Church still has its tradition of apophaticism, of describing God by saying what God is *not*: a helpful counterbalance to our very human desire to want to be endlessly putting into words what we think God is. Here are some fifth-century words, from Dionysius (or Denys) the Areopagite, whose writings were one of the bases of medieval theology:

> He who is the pre-eminent cause of all things intelligently perceived is not himself any of those things. . . . He is neither soul nor intellect; nor has He imagination, opinion, reason,

or understanding; nor can He be expressed or conceived, since He is neither number, nor order; nor greatness, nor smallness, nor equality, nor inequality; nor similarity, nor dissimilarity; neither is He standing, nor moving, nor at rest; neither has He power, nor is power, nor is light; neither does He live, nor is He life; neither is He essence, nor eternity, nor time; nor is He subject to intelligible contact; nor is He science, nor truth, nor kingship, nor wisdom; neither one, nor oneness; nor godhead, nor goodness; nor is He spirit according to our understanding, nor filiation, nor paternity; nor anything else known to us or to any other beings, of the things that are or the things that are not; neither does anything that is, know Him as He is; nor does He know existing things according to existing knowledge; neither can the reason attain to Him, nor name Him, nor know Him; neither is He darkness nor light, nor the false, nor the true; nor can any affirmation or negation be applied to Him, for although we may affirm or deny the things below Him, we can neither affirm nor deny Him, inasmuch as the all-perfect and unique Cause of all things transcends all affirmation, and the simple pre-eminence of His absolute nature is outside of every negation — free from every limitation and beyond them all.[2]

The twentieth-century theologian Paul Tillich says that most of our religious life is based on a human-created God:

The condition of man's relation to God is first of all one of *not* having, *not* seeing, *not* knowing, and *not* grasping. A religion in which that is forgotten, no matter how ecstatic or active or reasonable, replaces God by its own creation of an image of God. Our religious life is characterized more by that kind of creation than anything else.[3]

If the western Church had continued to share that tradition of the *via negativa*, or had even given more attention to the practice of wordless and image-less contemplative prayer, we might have a healthier fear of saying too much. Of course the Church started well enough:

God was pure mystery, the Church argued, and then set out to define the cosmos, creation, and the afterlife with a kind of precision at least audacious if not embarrassing. When human understanding of the cosmos changed and creation began to look like evolution, it took years, centuries, for the Church to accept the fact that the Holy Spirit was speaking in languages not theological.[4]

The people who sit in church on Sunday do not, in the main, read the works of theologians. They depend for their understanding of God on their own experience, on their reading of the Bible, on catechisms and any other such religious education they had in childhood, and on the words spoken from the altar or the pulpit by someone ordained or licensed to do so. So if they are, for example members of the Church of Ireland they will probably believe that God is "maker of heaven and earth"; is "our heavenly father" and "the giver of all goodness"; and is the author of "God's Commandments [which] God spake in the twentieth chapter of Exodus". They will also know that their duty towards God is:

> . . . to believe in him, to fear him, and to love him with all my heart, with all my mind, with all my soul, and with all my strength; to worship him, to give him thanks, to put my whole trust in him, to call upon him, to honour his holy name and his Word, and to serve him truly all the days of my life.

The Catechism of the Catholic Church, on the other hand, contains many pages about the One God and many more about God the Father, before even approaching the subjects of God the Son and God the Holy Spirit. Paragraph headings tell us that God is merciful and gracious, God is truth and love, God alone *is*.

> God is the fullness of Being and of every perfection, without origin and without end. All creatures receive all that they are and have from him; but he alone *is* his very being and he is of himself everything that he is.[5]

That might have been enough to say. But in the Catechism of the Catholic Church, there is much, much more. However, it includes the following:

> Since our knowledge of God is limited, our language about him is equally so . . . We must therefore continually purify our language of everything in it that is limited, image-bound or imperfect, if we are not to confuse our image of God — "the inexpressible, the incomprehensible, the invisible, the ungraspable"[6] — with our human representations. Our human words always fall short of the mystery of God.[7]

To describe, to name, is to have power over the creature that is named. In some cultures, it is not done to tell your name to a stranger until you know and trust them, because they might use that knowledge to have control over you. Adam's naming of the creatures of the earth, in chapter two of the Book of Genesis, is no doubt part of his taking that "dominion" over them that the Lord had promised in chapter one (even though the chapters were written several hundred years apart). There is that great refusal, in the Jewish scriptures, to name God, preferring instead to use a phrase meaning "God's name". All of this raises the question: if we are saying anything more than is necessary about God, are we not trying to take control of God? At first that seems laughable. But again and again in films and stories we learn that what is unknown is frightening. Once the wild creature in the forest has been seen, named, fed and tamed it is nothing to be afraid of any more. It goes against our security senses to live with something we do not know. Only the non-acquisitive or the wise can live with that unknowing. Yet that which we call God is essentially beyond and above what that anonymous fourteenth-century author called "the cloud of unknowing". Any parts of God which we see and name and feed and tame are no longer God. We don't easily accept that, preferring to be like the small child who asks its mother if God is everywhere and, receiving a positive answer, claps its hand over a cup and says "Got him!".

All our doctrines about God, all our statements about the things of God, are a way of saying like children "Got him!" It is time for us to grow up. Deep inside our heads and hearts we each have different images of God, even though our Churches try through teaching and preaching to make them uniform. A lot of fun is made of the image of an old man with a long white beard as being what people imagine God to be like. Yet most clergy will be aware that a large number, possibly a majority of people, when they use the word "God" have a picture in their head of a man with rich brown hair and beard, lovely eyes, and a long robe. In a word, Jesus. A letter in *The Irish Times* recently said, "God actually is a human being, and one quite critical of religious institutions" — clearly a reference to Jesus. God = Jesus, full stop.

Our visual images of God are heavily influenced by paintings and stained glass, mainly medieval (God) and nineteenth century (Jesus). The depiction of the Holy Spirit as a dove seems to have taken less of a hold on us, perhaps because it is difficult to imagine having a conversation with a large white bird; and so the twentieth century pendulum swing towards emphasis on the Spirit has been very much in terms of its being the power of God, whatever the creeds say about the Spirit being the third "person" of the Trinity.

So if we talk together about God, we probably have some very different images of God in our heads. Similarly, our relationship with that image varies a great deal, reflecting our way of relating to the humans in our lives, and influenced by the way those who taught us related to *their* image of God. Therefore it may range from being crawlingly deferential and fearful to lovingly feisty and challenging. God may be felt to be primarily a parent, or a spirit-guide, a powerful overlord or an encouraging teacher. The relationship may have elements of emotional sexuality in it. As it is very difficult for any of us to move beyond a sense of the maleness of God, and even though we are told that none of us is one hundred per cent heterosexual, this emotional sexuality may go some way towards accounting for the preponderance of women in our churches. Perhaps it also accounts for the significant number of gay men in the priesthood.

As well as what we hear from the Bible, the words we use in our liturgies and hymns also influence us. "Heavenly Father"; "Merciful Father"; "Lord" (this sometimes means God, sometimes Jesus); "God our Lord"; "Lord Jesus"; and (but rarely) "Lord and giver of life, Holy Spirit". The simple word "Father" seems the prevalent form of address in Roman Catholic prayers. The majority of Anglican prayers, at least in Ireland, still begin with that very nineteenth-century phrase, "Almighty God". The less feudal "Eternal God" seems to be gaining ground in England. In books of prayers compiled by women of all denominations, more original names, often based on the idea of God as nurturer, come through: "Dear God", "Loving God", "Gracious God", "Tender God", "God of light" and, of course, "Mother God".

And yet we do know, somewhere in the back of our heads, that God is not a person. Not a person, and not a thing. That was the great contribution of the theologian Paul Tillich, telling us that God is not a thing. And that point was taken up by Bishop John Robinson in his book *Honest to God*, published in 1963. The sensation that the book caused, and the calls for his resignation that it brought, were not because what he was saying was new. On the fortieth anniversary of the book's publication, a London clergyman and lecturer in philosophy has written:

> Why all the fuss? I think, precisely because [the book] was accessible. Professional religious types, clerical or academic, may shrug it off as so much regurgitated Tillich, Bultmann, and Bonhoeffer, but it was news to the people in the pews. The God of Sunday school, the God too many clergy had refused to challenge for fear of giving offence, was in the process of being gently dismantled. God, accord-

ing to Robinson, is not any sort of thing. Things are pro-
scribed and limited; things appeal to us because they are
essentially graspable. But God is beyond human graspabil-
ity. . . . Throughout the ages, mystical writers have tried to
strip us of confidence that we can grasp the essence of God
. . . The God that is a thing is an idol of human contrivance.[8]

One of the oldest problems of religion is how the existence of God
can be compatible with the presence of suffering and evil in the
world. For most people, to believe in God is to pray for the bad
things to be averted from them and from those they love. But the
bad things happen, and with apparently unaccountable random-
ness. There are many answers to the questions, "Why does God
allow suffering?" and "Why has God allowed this to happen to
me/him/her/them?". They vary from "Otherwise no-one would
ever die and the world would be full to bursting point in a few
years", to "Evil must be allowed free rein or our choice of God/
good would be meaningless", to "Your prayer for so-and-so was
answered: the answer was No". Such answers satisfy few. This
problem is not confined to Christianity. A Jewish writer says:

> Holocaust Memorial Day . . . is a time for reflection and
> prayer, yet it raises fundamental problems about the nature
> and activity of God. Where was God when six million
> died? . . . The time has come to undertake a radical revision
> of both Jewish and Christian theology. . . . The varied truth-
> claims of the world's religions must be regarded as human
> images, which are constructed from within particular social
> and cultural contexts. . . .[9] - -from "A mystery beyond our
> by Cohn-Shebok" conception"

The only alternatives seem to be to say either that God contains
both good and bad (which very few are comfortable with) or to
say that we have got it wrong all these years and that God is not,
after all, all-powerful. But that is also unsatisfactory as it appears
to limit God to something less than an efficient caretaker of creation. The best answer may lie in the realisation that death is both

inevitable and necessary; and that it is not God but often we ourselves, through our actions, and our failures to act, and also through the functioning of our unconscious, who are responsible for the world's ills.

The idea that God can do anything if we pray hard enough is tempting, but dangerous. The religious education of children commonly includes the idea that if only we can trust sufficiently in God then God will be able to save us from all unpleasantness and horrid happenings. Since few churches provide much in the way of ongoing or adult religious education, far too many people get stuck at that childhood level of understanding. And then when something bad happens to them, when some tragedy strikes in life — even if it is something as common and natural as the death of an elderly parent or sibling or spouse — their faith in God may easily collapse. They feel betrayed: if not openly, then, at least in their heads, they are saying: "I prayed for him/her; I've always tried to lead a decent life; how can this have been allowed to happen?" We need to educate ourselves into a less superstitious and more religious faith, so that by drawing God into such situations we can cope with tragedy and grief in ways that help us to grow rather than destroying us.

So behind the simple word "God" we have all these very personal images and expectations of God. And unless we are spiritually deadened our view of God changes with our life experiences. The "truth" about God differs for each one of us according to our experience of God, which is affected by our experience of life and other relationships. Much as the organisational Church would like to have us all tidily believing one "truth", it is not humanly possible as long as we acknowledge that God is way beyond the little that we can grasp. So it is not a question of whether what seems to you to be the truth is right or wrong, but only whether it is honestly the best truth at which you can arrive. (We will look at this subject in more detail in Chapter Seven.)

Do we need the word "God" at all? Some post-Christians are saying now that we should drop the idea that there is any sort of Being beyond ourselves, and concentrate on recognising "the transcendent" whenever and wherever we can, as we can in music, and art, and nature, and in love. Such recognition is vitally important. Yet I believe that most people who acknowledge some sort of religious or spiritual experience (which the majority of people are said to have had) will affirm that there is something personal in it, some sense of having been in contact with another being, another identity, a "presence" which is relating specifically to them. People who pray are similarly convinced of a "presence" that relates to them, and that is indeed very valid, though less conclusive. Because in praying to God we may to some extent be casting God in the image of a beloved parent or teacher or pastor, and getting responses that are bounced back from our understanding of how that particular model would have responded. The evidence of those out-of-the-ordinary but often out-of-the-blue religious experiences, on the other hand, are more objectively convincing.

Many have said that some sense of a higher or greater presence is built into us as human beings. Scientific evidence is suggesting that religion, even belief in a Supreme Being, is a physical part of us, in the same way that the desire to eat or to have sex is part of our biological programming. This is convincing because it would explain the persistence of religious faith when everything combines to suggest that it should have died out long ago. Our ideas about God have shifted so much over the centuries that it is as if the human race has been willing to let go of various definitions of God (or whatever other name they use for a divine or ultimate Being), one by one, but always holds on to the basic idea. A good example in Christian terms is "the God of the gaps", an expression that was very popular a few decades ago. It meant that in the infancy of humanity, thunderstorms and others terrors of nature were thought to be directly caused by the anger of God. When scientific understanding grew, that idea of God was abandoned, and so in time were other gap ideas of God. So that, as Dietrich Bonhoeffer wrote, God was constantly being pushed back, was continually in retreat. As science grew, so the number of mysterious things attributed to God shrunk. This will undoubtedly continue. The scientist Richard Dawkins refers to ". . . the Einstein/Hawking trick of letting 'God' stand for 'That which we don't understand'", and adds:

> It would be a harmless trick if it were not continually misunderstood by those hungry to misunderstand it. In any case, optimists among scientists, of whom I am one, will insist that "That which we don't understand" means only "That which we don't *yet* understand". Science is still working on the problem.[10]

This implies that eventually the remaining God will be so small as to vanish entirely. But for Bonhoeffer, this was always the wrong way to go.

> We are to find God in what we know, not in what we don't know. . . . God is no stop-gap. He must be recognized at the centre of life, not when we are at the end of our resources.[11]

So the shrinking of the God of the gaps is not a sign that God as God is fading out of existence, but only that that account of God was always less than adequate. Reports of God's death have been frequent in history, but have always turned out to be exaggerated. Each time, what has gone is not God as God but some human description or definition of God, or attitude to God, that has become outworn and useless. Don Cupitt is one of the people who has written about this:

> It is possible for people, and even for a whole society, to lose faith in God. . . . It happens, not primarily because they have decided that something they used to think existed does not after all exist, but because the available language about God has been allowed to become too narrow, stale,

and spiritually obsolete, and no longer functions as a satisfactory vehicle through which people can articulate their
highest life-aims. The work of creative religious personali-
ties is continually to enrich, to enlarge and sometimes to
purge the available stock of religious symbols and idioms
so that faith in God shall continue to be possible.[12]

As long as we remember that all the words we say about God and
all the pictures we make of God are our own creations, then letting some of them go is no disaster. That which we call God is always greater than anything we can think, and greater than any of
our words or images concerning God, and will survive our efforts.

What complicates all this is that a very important part of
Christian doctrine is the concept of Revelation. This says that God
has revealed to us the truth about the character and purposes of
God, through events and through experience and through the in-
sights of theologians and others. In practice, this has meant that
claims by individuals to certain truths have always had to be examined by the Church before being accepted and promoted. So
from revelation comes doctrine, and thus the vastness of God is
fitted into small boxes of human words. From there, it is only a
small step to "God" becoming a human construct, an idol, while
the reality of God escapes our boxes and is free. Our way out of
this is already available to us: the recognition that Revelation is
not something that only happened to great people in the past, but
is something that is always happening, continuously. When Jesus'
followers were distressed at the prospect of losing him, he re-
minded them that even when he was gone, God's spirit would
come to them and guide them.

But if God is mystery, and way beyond us, then surely models
and images of God are necessary for us who are only human?
They may be so, but they must not be set in concrete. They must
be fluid, ephemeral, good for as long as they are helpful and then
discarded. As the Catholic priest Adrian B. Smith says:

No one image of the Divine can be final or all-embracing when a human being tries to grasp the concept of God. The Lord's Prayer was only introduced into Christian liturgy in the third century but because the Church has retained the concept of God as "Our Father" in its worship ever since, we might be led to believe that this revelation — coming from Jesus as it did — was the ultimate stage of our spiritual evolution. It is not. It was simply the next stage which was appropriate two thousand years ago. The Church's teaching has frozen Jesus' words for all time and in all cultures, forgetting that he was a man of his own times and culture. It was not meant to be the ultimate nor the total expression of Godhead. . . . With the development of the behavioural sciences we understand that maturity calls for us to go beyond the child–parent dependency to an adult-to-adult relationship between people. To get stuck at the level of the Father–child relationship to God can become a form of idolatry. We would be transforming what is no more than a model into a reality. It is not even a model that appeals to everyone. For someone who in their childhood suffered abuse from their father or step-father, or indeed never knew a father, this model can be a real obstacle.[13]

The danger of any sort of set-in-concrete human-made model is that it may fail. Then we need to be ready to see that it is the model that has failed, not God. Every model is liable to let us down. Only a God who is always greater than anything we can think can support all our projections, absorb all our expectations, and still be there. Which is why our images of God, though necessary, will need to be as large and exterior and unbounded as possible — the Unknown God which Paul refers to in Acts 17 — and as small and interior as possible — the "still small voice" that Elijah heard in 1 Kings 19. The same Paul Tillich who said that God was not a thing also helped many people by his image of God as depth, as "the ground of our being".

> . . . if you know that God means depth you know much
> about him. You cannot then call yourself an atheist or unbe-
> liever. For you cannot think or say: Life has no depth! Life
> is shallow.[14]

Through the centuries, the mystics have come closest to giving us
non-concrete ways to free up our minds and hearts in the seeking
of God. Yet the word "mysticism" presents a problem to the
twenty-first century. It has been proposed by Professor Denys
Turner that somewhere during the nineteenth century it came to
mean an *experiencing* of God that brings happiness and a sense of
eternity; that this understanding of it continued through the twentieth century; and that the period we are now living in, postmod-
ernism, is more open to the original mind of the early mystics. To
them God was not something to be experienced and enjoyed by
the individual self, but the opposite: God was to be met by the
soul in darkness, unknowableness, absence. Turner writes:

> Modern interpretation has invented "mysticism" and . . .
> we persist in reading back the terms of that conjection upon
> a stock of mediaeval authorities who knew of no such thing
> — or, when they knew of it, decisively rejected it.[15]

This is a valuable insight, with much food for the Christianity of
the future. Keeping it in mind, we can look to the riches of the
past. "A deep but dazzling darkness" is the seventeenth-century
poet Henry Vaughan's image of God. In the twentieth century,
Anthony Bloom of the Russian Orthodox Church talked of "the
absence that is a presence", and the poet R.S. Thomas often used
the same phrase: "It is this great absence / that is like a presence,
that compels / me to address it without hope / of a reply . . . What
resource have I / other than the emptiness without him of my
whole / being, a vacuum he may not abhor?" Julian of Norwich, in
the fourteenth century, was six hundred years ahead of Tillich's
emphasis on the "ground of our being" when she wrote these as-
tounding and beautiful words:

God is nearer to us than our own soul, for he is the ground in which it stands, and he is the means by which substance and sensuality are so held together that they can never separate. Our soul reposes in God its true rest, and stands in God, its true strength, and is fundamentally rooted in God, its eternal love.[16]

Jesus, Christ

"The Lord is our God, the Lord alone. You shall love the Lord your God with all your heart, and with all your soul, and with all your might." (Moses)

"The Lord our God, the Lord is one; you shall love the Lord with all your heart, and with all your soul, and with all your mind, and with all your strength." (Jesus)

For twenty-first-century Christians, the question of what we believe about Jesus is the subject which most urgently needs to be examined. Some of the urgency comes from our increasing relationship with the other monotheistic world faiths: those which believe there is only one God. We are in an uncomfortable position when we talk with representatives of Judaism and Islam, and insist that we believe there are three "persons" in that one God. A Muslim writer has said:

The concept of *tawhid* is the very essence of Islam. It refers to the affirmation of the Oneness of God. . . . The Koran teaches that the prophets were sent by God to remind all nations of this truth and to urge them to avoid the grave sin of *shirk*, the association of partners with God. It is no coincidence that Moses and Jesus taught that observing the *shema*, the Hebrew equivalent of *tawhid*, was the most important commandment of all (Deuteronomy 6:4, Mark 12:29). In the Islamic world, all beliefs contrary to *tawhid* represent a falling away from that original monotheism. . . . Muslims since the time of the Prophet [Mohammed] have been critical of trinitarian Christianity for postulating three persons in the godhead, each of whom is "fully God" according to the Nicene Creed. They assert that this represents a deviation from clear prophetic teachings. . . . Mohammed's success was to re-establish the pure faith of his forefather Abraham by emphatically insisting that worship should not be directed towards anyone except God alone, and that no-one else should be the object of adoration or fear.[17]

But even apart from interfaith relations, the status of Jesus is the area where the difference in thinking between the first and the twenty-first centuries is widest. The basic problem is that traditionally Christians have held that the first-century person we know as Jesus is in some way the same as the being we call God. "Jesus is Lord", we say or sing; "the only-begotten Son of God". The meaning is clear: "I believe that Jesus is divine".

To begin with, maybe it helps to recognise that when phrases like this are said, they are bundling together two different ideas about Jesus. One is the equating of a human being with that which is divine, or non-human. The other is what is felt to be the continuing presence with us of this particular person: "Jesus is Lord" and "Jesus is divine" are both spoken in the present tense.

To take that last idea first: it is an important aspect of Christianity to be able to address Jesus in thought or in prayer, and to sense some sort of contact with him, perhaps in the way of support or guidance or simply of love. Such communication does not depend on Jesus being divine. Many people admit, often quite shyly, to having an ongoing relationship with people they have loved but who have died: "I still say goodnight to her every night." It doesn't matter that we have no actual knowledge of what happens after death: the continuing sense of relationship is apparently a very human response to the death of a loved one. And it seems to be effective: it helps the bereaved and can be a source of guidance. If it can work with a spouse or a grandparent, it can work also with Jesus, a person whose character and teaching we have some considerable knowledge of from the Bible, and who from reading about we grow to love.

The other idea about Jesus, that although he was a human being he is to be equated with that which is God — which is to say non-human — is one that causes serious problems for thinking people in this time. It is very much a first-century concept. At that stage of the world's development, many people, not even just a select few, were considered to be gods, or fathered by one of the gods: the Greek myths in particular are full of such stories. Closer to Jesus' homeland, the despised Canaanite religion contained similar ideas. We no longer have the sort of minds which can take that in in a mythical or metaphorical sense and at the same time accept it as fact. But looking back, we can see how the story of Jesus was fitted into such thinking. December 25 was the birthday of the Phrygian sun god Attis. Later it was to be the birthday of another god: Mithras, the Persian sun god. He also was born of a virgin and resurrected after death. In the fourth century, December 25 was declared to be the birthday of Jesus. All those other stories of divine births have been abandoned as the world grew; the Christian one was retained. For political reasons in the fourth century, the Church had set it in concrete in the creeds, so it could not easily be cast off. The Emperor had begun to wear his invisible new clothes.

So we need to ask: What does it mean to say that Jesus is God? Leaving aside the fourth-century politicking, what lay behind this way of describing him? That a human being is God is not a fact as such, certainly not a verifiable fact. A human being is of a different order of existence from that which we call God. If it is not a fact, then it was a way of *saying something*. And if we can reach back to that something, perhaps we can find new ways of stating it that are compatible with our twenty-first-century understanding of people, of history, of holiness and of God.

It is difficult to know precisely when those who knew Jesus in the flesh began to equate him with God. We may even have to ask *whether* they did, at that time, or if this was something that developed a generation or so later. The first parts of our New Testament to be written were the letters of Paul, and he had not known Jesus in person. The Gospels, with the numerous sayings on which ideas of Jesus' divinity were hung, such as Peter saying to Jesus, "You are the Christ, the Son of the living God", were written much later. Mark's gospel was probably written about thirty-five years after the death of Jesus, and John's possibly sixty years after. Rather than factual recordings made at the time, they were collections of events and sayings put together from memories and from stories told down through the years. Many of them would have grown and had other incidents, and theological statements, grafted on in the telling, before the Canon of the New Testament (the defining of certain books as inspired writing) was settled in the fourth century.

In order to find the truth about Jesus, we have to put our minds back into the past, as far as that is possible at all, and read the documents we have as if we were reading a detective story. What is going on here? What is the *most likely* reason for this, or that? If we feel that no human being can be also the non-human reality that we call God, then why, at that time when such liaisons were taken for granted, was Jesus described in that way? What was it about him? The one consistent factor in all the tellings was that this man was godly. Through his preaching and teaching and through his healing of people, Jesus was experienced as being closer to God than anyone else his followers had ever known. But it is almost incredible that they, with their Jewish upbringing, would ever during his lifetime have thought of him as God. The idea would surely have horrified them. John Hick writes:

> The following picture can only reflect what I personally regard as the most reliable New Testament scholarship since the critical rediscovery of the Jewishness of Jesus in the 1970s. . . . He felt called by God . . . It did not however amount to his being God incarnate. Jesus did not think of himself as God, and can have had no conception of the later

Christian doctrine according to which he was the second person of a divine trinity. This would have been impossible to a faithful Jew. "Why do you call me good?" he is reported to have said, "No one is good but God alone."(Mark 10:18)[18]

That is from a fairly recent book. But 25 years ago, the Church of Ireland bishop Richard Hanson was saying that even then such thinking was nearly a century old:

In [the Gospels of Matthew, Mark and Luke] Jesus does not say that he is God, does not occupy almost all his discourses speaking about his own person, claims no pre-existence. . . . The scholars have their explanation of this of course, one apparently unknown to the believers and the clergy, though it has been current and available for nearly a hundred years now. The first three gospels give us, roughly speaking, the best historical account of Jesus that we have. The Gospel of John is less an historical account than a theological commentary on the significance of Jesus. . . . The great majority of clergy of all denominations seem either to be unaware of modern scholarly opinion about St John's Gospel, or are engaged in a conspiracy of silence to say nothing about it, and are content to assist their people to continue in ignorance of what must be, on any estimate, a vitally important fact for contemporary Christianity.[19]

More recently, Clare Richards, writing for those studying Roman Catholic theology for the Catholic Certificate in Religious Studies, examines various titles used of Jesus, such as Lord, Word of God, Son of Man, Saviour, and shows that none of them say that Jesus is God. She unwraps the heading "Son of God" in this way:

Son of God is a metaphor used through the Old Testament for angels, Israel, kings, the virtuous, and any son or daughter of Adam. All these usages entitle Jesus to be called "Son of God". . . . Jesus' followers happily see him as the model of sonship of God, but they know that they, too,

must be conformed to that image (cf. Romans 8:29; Gala-
tians 4:6, 8:29; 1 John 3:1). To speak of Jesus as "divine"
does not *add* anything to his humanness. He is Son of God
by being the *man* he is, in whom we see (undistorted) the
face of God.

Later she asks whether it would not be sensible to "accept a certain plurality in Christology" (the study of Christ), since all models used in theology are incomplete.[20]

Jesus was experienced in his own time as being close to God.
But the pivotal event, the event that created Christianity, was
clearly his death and what happened after it. Imagine yourself
back into those times and you can see that to have your beloved
leader and spiritual guide suddenly taken from you and killed
would be the most terrible shock. You would be stunned; you
would hide away for a time. But then, because there were many of
you, the common will to survive would assert itself. You might
find yourself saying, as bereaved people often do, "But it's alright.
I can still feel him with me. I hear his voice. He is guiding me. *He
is still here!*" And with a large number of you feeling and then saying that, the communal reaction to loss would swell up into joy.
The knowledge that communication with the one who has died
has not ceased might well lead from "hearing" and sensing to reports of "seeing" Jesus. "Did not our hearts burn within us, while
he talked with us?", the words of the two apostles on the road
from Emmaus, after the stranger has talked with them, broken
bread with them and then gone on his way, give a movingly clear
picture of people reading their deepest desires into an event.

Most people are enlarged by their death. Whether they have
been just someone in the community, or a friend or family member, or a well-known celebrity, from the moment of their death
they become a story. Within days, and particularly at the funeral,
the story-telling begins. "She had never a day's illness in her life
till the end"; "Do you remember when he bought the old horse?";
"She would do anything for anyone"; "We'll never see anyone like

him again". From the moment of death, that person is placed securely in the past. He or she can be summed up now. The stories can be told because they will not be contradicted by any future behaviour of the deceased. And of course, the greater or more charismatic the person, the larger the stories. The death of the English princess, Diana, showed fascinatingly how public grief can make a near-saint out of a very human woman. In the Church, the good person who also has a charisma about them may gather after their death so many tales of holiness and miracles that in time there may come calls for him/her to be declared a saint. Jesus, after his death, could be spoken of entirely in terms of his wisdom, his goodness, his godliness. His followers would have dredged their memories for every word he had ever said, and would have endlessly repeated them, especially when they gathered together to talk about him and to figure out what they were going to do now to keep his teachings alive and honour his hopes for them. The effect of their gatherings, even while they were still practising Jews, would have been to glorify the figure of Jesus, not least to counteract any public tendency to write him off as an executed criminal. Names such as "the Lord", "the Son of God", "the Christ" (i.e. the anointed one), would have been increasingly used of him.

In those meetings to break bread together, to repeat Jesus' teachings and to await what they understood to be his promised return, the Christian Church was born. We are talking about a period from the fourth decade of the first century to its close.

As we have seen, it was about 200 years later, in 325 AD, that the Nicene Creed was issued in its first form. The modern version is given at the start of Chapter Two, but the old sixteenth-century version is still in use in many churches. In that form, it says of Jesus:

> . . . One Lord Jesus Christ, the only-begotten Son of God,
> begotten of his Father before all worlds, God of God, Light
> of Light, Very God of Very God, begotten not made, being
> of one substance with the Father, by whom all things were
> made: who for us men, and for our salvation came down

from heaven, and was incarnate by the Holy Ghost of the Virgin Mary, and was made man, and was crucified also for us under Pontius Pilate. He suffered and was buried, and the third day he rose again according to the Scriptures, and ascended into heaven, and sitteth on the right hand of the Father. And he shall come again with glory to judge both the quick and the dead: whose kingdom shall have no end.

It is interesting to note that the original 325 AD version was briefer:

... One Lord Jesus Christ, the Word of God, God from God, Light from Light, Life from Life, Only-begotten Son, first-born of all creation, before all the ages begotten from the Father, by whom also all things were made; who for our salvation was incarnate, and lived among men, and suffered, and rose again the third day, and ascended to the Father, and will come again in glory to judge living and dead.

It is even more interesting to learn that it was not theologians or clergy who altered it but the emperor of that time ("our most pious emperor", "our most wise and religious emperor", as the contemporary writer Eusebius called him) who wanted changes made. So the authors of the Creed produced this version, which was accepted:

... One Lord Jesus Christ, the Son of God, begotten of the Father, Only-begotten, that is, from the substance of the Father; God from God, Light from Light, Very God from Very God, begotten not made, Consubstantial with the Father, by whom all things were made, both things in heaven and things on earth; who for us men, and for our salvation came down and was incarnate, was made man, suffered, and rose again the third day, ascended into heaven, and is coming to judge living and dead.

The words that we now use, which were added much later, are:

> . . . [was incarnate] by the Holy Ghost of the Virgin Mary
> . . . and was crucified also for us under Pontius Pilate . . .
> was buried . . . [rose again] according to the Scriptures, . . .
> and sitteth on the right hand of the Father . . . [shall come
> again] with glory . . . whose kingdom shall have no end.

So neither Mary nor Pontius Pilate were part of the original. On the other hand, all versions contain the phrase or phrases "only-begotten Son", "Son of God", or "only-begotten Son of God". About this, Adrian B. Smith says:

> Perhaps the most important New Testament title for Jesus is "Son of God". At least it is for us as we understand the expression with all the theological weight which it has gathered over the Christian centuries. But we have to realise that it did not originally have the meaning in Hebrew culture which we commonly give it in the Church. Among the Chosen People, the title was given to an individual or group who was close to God, under God's protection. The Jewish nation as a whole was called God's Son (Psalm 2:7), as was a devout believer. In a special way the title belonged to the King of Israel (2 Samuel 7:14). When the title is applied to Jesus in the New Testament Letter to the Hebrews — "You are my Son; today I have become your Father" (1:5 and 5:4-5) — it is in this same sense, as a specially chosen person. So to describe Jesus as "Son of God" was to speak of his significance rather than to account for his origins. Only after the Council of Nicaea in the 4th century did the phrase take on the Trinitarian meaning we give it today in the Creed as "only begotten Son of God". In fact at Nicaea, the phrase "Son of God" was promoted to mean "God the Son".[21]

By the time this Nicene formula of faith was drawn up, many generations had passed since those who had known Jesus had been still alive. All that could be known about him had to be gained from tradition and from the many documents that had been written about him, mostly from 50 AD to 90 AD, although only from those which the Church had approved.

Then in 451 AD, a century and a quarter after the working out of the Nicene Creed, a number of powerful Christians met at a place called Chalcedon to counteract the many and various different ideas about Jesus that were flying about. In order to hold together the political-ecclesiastical structures of the time, authoritarian statements had to be made. Chalcedon produced the Declaration that Jesus was "one Person in two Natures", human and divine. This was more than three hundred years after the death of Jesus. We would laugh now at the idea of putting into official words beliefs that people had been formulating in 1700 AD. Even if we allow for the likelihood that human understanding has accelerated in recent centuries, we would find it hard to assent to much of the thinking of even one hundred and fifty years ago. It would be akin to our saying now that there is nothing wrong with slavery. That is one possible contemporary reaction to such a Declaration. Another might be of sadness that the beautiful Jesus from Nazareth who had gone about healing people and showing a God of love was made over into a philosophical concept about which people argued and, later, killed. Bishop Hugh Montefiore has said that the Chalcedon definition of the two natures of Christ no longer works.

> This ancient Definition, for all the authority that it carries, is no longer credible as it stands in today's world. . . . In a famous phrase, it was remarked that it represents "the bankruptcy of Greek patristic theology".[22] It must be respected because it preserved in its day the kernel of the Gospel. But we can no longer accept it as an explanation of the mystery of Jesus' person which rings true for us today.[23]

The bishop now believes that Christianity has been too dogmatic, and needs to allow divergent interpretations of the events on which it is built.[24]

Within the culture of the early Church, the divinising of Jesus must have been a great support as the Christian community separated from Judaism. That support and encouragement presumably went on, in the Mediterranean area and what we now call Europe, into the Middle Ages, when belief in magic was still a part of everyday life. But with the fifteenth, sixteenth, seventeenth and especially eighteenth centuries, that changed. And since then this basic and central Christian doctrine has been on the defensive. For hundreds of years it was only the intellectuals, whether educated or uneducated, who could allow themselves *not* to say that the Emperor had a marvellous suit of clothes.

What place then, does Jesus have in an honest Christianity? What does he mean to us in the third millennium? Can we find a new way of expressing the reflection of God that people saw in him?

Most of us, I think, will accept the idea that there is something of God in everyone. Whatever we know or don't know about the historical Jesus, it is clear that in him many of the people of his time saw the working of God in a way they had seen in no other. So perhaps we can say this: in all people there is at least a little bit of God; in some people there is a lot of God; and in some a great amount of God. In Jesus there was *so much* of God that those who came in contact with him could not see where Jesus stopped and God began. But it did not mean he was God. God was in Jesus, but God is more than Jesus: that is to say, Jesus is not all that God is. Theologian John Macquarrie says:

> I believe that to some extent God's image remains vestigially in every human being, but the Christian claim is that in Christ Jesus that image has clearly shone forth. . . . [T]he difference between Christ and other human beings is one of degree, rather than of kind.[25]

And Hugh Montefiore also talks about the similarities and the differences between the human Jesus and us:

> If our experience of grace is only fitful and fragmentary, and if Jesus' commitment, as we see it in the Gospels, was total and complete, there is a vast qualitative distinction

between him and us which does not remove his real humanity and kinship with us.[26]

It was Jesus' godliness that led the early Church to describe him
as part of God. We in our time can acknowledge that way of hon-
ouring him without taking it literally; though we will need to
change some of the words we say about Jesus so that others will
not think we mean it literally.

To allow ourselves to think of Jesus as truly one of us, human
without being divine, is not necessarily a loss. For many, the honest acknowledgement of what they have for a long time half
thought brings the unexpected delight of renewed devotion to one
of the most beautiful figures the world has ever known. As the
Benedictine Joan Chittister says:

> I believe that in the humanity of Jesus lies the glory of us
> all. The thought is awesome in its implications for lives lost
> in the humdrum, weighed down by depression, dulled to
> the divinity around them, and discouraged by their own
> limitations. If Jesus is the Breath of the Spirit, if the Spirit
> can work through the humanity of Jesus, then the Spirit can
> work through our humanity, as well. Humanity is not in-
> imical to holiness. The flesh is not evil. Then, the connec-
> tion between flesh and spirit makes miracles of us all.[27]

In some Christian circles, it is important to say that Jesus is or was
unique. In the sense that every human being is unique, then of
course he was. But if they mean that he was uniquely the source of
salvation, and that only Christians can be "saved", that is altogether a different matter. First we need to know what "salvation"
means to the person asking the question. Is it wholeness and
health? For some, the influence of Christianity has led to quite the
opposite of wholeness and health. Is it life after death? If that is
salvation we have no way of knowing if it has been achieved. Altogether I believe the use of the word "unique" in connection with
Jesus is meaningless. And unpleasant: it implies that Christianity is

superior to every other world faith, that Christians have some sort of priority with God. These are views that are quietly being dropped. The theologian Norman Pittenger said thirty years ago: "The fact is that the word [unique] has become so highly ambiguous in recent discussion that it might better be avoided altogether." He wrote about Professor C. Moule's distinction between two ways of looking at uniqueness. "Uniqueness of exclusion" meant that, with regard to Jesus, no parallels or similarities were permitted; "uniqueness of inclusion" could include qualities which have been found elsewhere but in a much less adequate fashion.

> If we follow this usage, it is apparent from the New Testament that the uniqueness of Jesus is of inclusion rather than exclusion. . . . To say that an event is absolutely different is really to say that it is not properly human or historical in any sense which can be defended if we are to talk in terms of the NT material. Those who speak about Jesus in this way have permitted themselves to adopt, albeit unconsciously, a Christological position which effectively removes him from the context of the historical situation in which he made his appearance.[28]

In short, if Jesus was unique, he would not have been properly human. This is close to the ancient heresy of docetism, the belief that Jesus only *appeared* to be human and to suffer.

There is a lot to be done. We probably need to distinguish between the names Jesus (the first-century man) and Christ (his spirit among us now). We need a new way of expressing the significance of the death of Jesus without all that unpleasant medieval talk about his blood buying our freedom. We need a way to let go of terms like "virgin birth" and "bodily resurrection" that have been connected with Jesus, but at the same time to reclaim and re-express the wonderful seasons of Christmas and Easter in our communities. We need to be confident that the word "Christian" can be applied to us and to all who want to explore and follow the teachings of Jesus.

Indeed, the theologian Paul Tillich was writing over fifty years ago that "the call of Jesus" is the one important thing:

> Jesus is not the creator of another religion, but the victor over religion. He is not the Maker of another law, but the conqueror of law. We, the ministers and teachers of Christianity, do not call you to Christianity but rather to the New Being to which Christianity should be a witness and nothing else, not confusing itself with that New Being. Forget all Christian doctrines; forget your own certainties and your own doubts, when you hear the call of Jesus. Forget all Christian morals, your achievements and your failures, when you come to Him. Nothing is demanded of you — no idea of God, and no goodness in yourselves, not your being religious, not your being Christian, not your being wise, and not your being moral. But what is demanded is only your being open and willing to accept what is given to you, the New Being, the being of love and justice and truth, as it is manifest in Him whose yoke is easy and whose burden is light.

Basically, we need to "let go and let God": let go of our desire for left-brain, analytical, rational, scientific certainty in matters of faith, and let the spirit of God lead us into new ways of just and loving and creative freedom.

The Virgin Birth

The question of the divinity of Jesus does not of course rest on the verifiability of what we have called "the Virgin Birth"; that is, on whether divine action took the place of the male part of Jesus' conception or whether he had an unacknowledged human father. That would be to look at it the wrong way around. The concept of the Incarnation — of God entering that particular human life in a unique way — was something that grew in later decades and was then written into the gospels when they were set down. In other words, once Jesus was seen to have been divine, at least two of the five major New Testament writers found it appropriate to include

a suitable birth narrative in their writings. Probably such narratives had been accumulating over the decades. But in fact the later
discovery of woman's part in conception, and more recently of the
chromosomes necessary to make a male child, put an end to the
making of new stories about virgin births. And there were such a
lot of these in the ancient world. Alexander the Great was said to
be divine, his mother impregnated variously by a thunderbolt or
by a serpent. The Emperor Augustus was described by the poet
Horace as the god Mercury incarnate. The words "Theos" (god)
and "Kyrios" (lord) were used of him. Romulus, the founder of
the city of Rome, was not only fathered by Mars, the god of war,
but also ended his life by ascending into the heavens. Julius Cae-
sar was described as "god made manifest" and "common saviour
of human life."[29]

All of this shows that it was not at all unusual in those times to
attribute divinity to great people. For the emerging Church to proclaim that Jesus, too, was divine must have helped in the gaining of
converts and the growth of Christianity through the first millennium and longer. This is not to suggest that it was a calculated de-
vice. Bishop John Spong, the former Episcopalian Bishop of
Newark, New Jersey, in his book *Why Christianity Must Change or
Die*, gives a brilliant account of how the early Christians, and Paul
in particular, struggled to interpret what they had seen of God in
Jesus. "Jesus had been for Paul the God-bearer, the human life
through which a new reality of God had been channelled." Drawing on ancient Jewish use of the word *nephesh* (later translated as
"soul" or "spirit") to indicate the breath of God dwelling within
humans, Spong says that for Paul Jesus was a "spirit person", a
God-presence. Paul's first letter to the young Church was written
around the year 50 or 51 of the Common Era (AD), some twenty
years after the death of Jesus; and the earliest gospel, Mark's, is
thought to come about fifteen years later than that. Neither speak of
Jesus as God; both speak of him as one who is full of the spirit of
God. It was the gospels of Matthew and Luke, written many dec-

ades later, which created the story of a miraculous birth, bringing
in symbols of ancient Jewish sacred stories such as the wise men,
the star, the shepherds and so on. They were not intended as literal
biography but were pointers to the significance of Jesus. Thus the
story of Jesus, with good intentions, became distorted.[30]

Now that we can see that Jesus' divinity is an assertion that
was a product of its time, but one that for some time has actually
been contributing to the decline of Christianity, we must have the
courage to let it go. One of the first books to say this clearly was
The Myth of God Incarnate, a series of essays by several serious and
respected English theologians published as long ago as 1977. In it,
Frances Young makes the point that the early Christians in their
response to Jesus felt "compelled" to find supernatural definitions
of him; but that that should not prevent us from expressing intelligently our own testimony to him. In another essay, Maurice
Wiles says it is more reasonable to see the doctrine of the Incarnation as an interpretation of Jesus appropriate to the age in which it
arose, rather than to treat it as an unalterable truth for all generations.[31] In a much later book summing up the whole subject of
Christology, theologian John Macquarrie lays aside the old ways
of talking of God coming down into a mortal body as Jesus:

> Virtually all modern theology has abandoned the idea of
> sudden irruptions from outside (the old supernaturalism,
> or God's action "vertically from above" . . .) . . . and sees
> things happening as gradual processes, though not without
> critical moments.[32]

This does not mean we can never again celebrate Christmas. The
birth narratives can become all the richer for us once we are able
to see them as multi-faceted reflections of light and truth rather
than as bald statements of questionable historical fact. Truth
comes to us by many avenues, and often most memorably and
powerfully by the indirect ways of poetry and novels. And that is
what the Christmas story is. Angels singing in a dark sky, the

warm breath of beasts around a manger, shepherds bringing lambs, kings or wise men following a star: all of these convey the arrival of a remarkable human being far more graphically than the cold statement of the time and place of his birth. These images of glory we can celebrate; and celebrate them all the more whole-heartedly for knowing we are not pretending to literal truth. And the message they are conveying and have always conveyed, the message that has always been understood by human hearts cele-brating Christmas, is that God is part of human life, is in it with us: that the divine and the human are bound up together and are everywhere to be found by those who have eyes to see them.

Mary

What of the significance of Mary as part of Jesus' story? There is no need to let go of that either. Our Christian tradition has little enough of the feminine. Attempts to use feminine language for the third person of the Trinity, the Holy Spirit, have generally failed, even though they follow on from the fact that Wisdom is referred to in the Old Testament as female, and the Hebrew word for the Spirit of God, *Ruach*, was also feminine. It has often been said that in some parts of the Christian Church, Mary has herself been elevated to divine level to fill that gap. Probably we have now moved beyond such relatively minor tinkerings and are in a space where we can more readily and helpfully conceive of God as either beyond maleness and femaleness or as containing both maleness and femaleness. But the figure of the mother of the man Jesus will always enrich our faith, with or without notions of a miraculous birth. A lot of our doctrine has hung on the word "virgin". We could ask a chicken-and-egg question: was virginity highly prized throughout most of the history of Christianity be-cause Mary was thought to have been a virgin at the time of the birth of Jesus, or was Mary described as being a virgin because virginity was in those times highly prized? Whether it was one way or both, it was necessary for the safe and peaceable running of society. That is, until the twentieth century brought reliable contraception for all who wanted it. Up until that time, virginity (and faithfulness within marriage) was necessary for at least two reasons. One was for the protection of women, in societies where there would be no-one to care for a young mother without a man. The other, especially where property was concerned, was to ensure inheritance through the male line. When a baby was born, it was important for the community to know who had fathered it.

However, all these arguments and discussions become unimportant when we realise, as scholars have for some time, that describing Mary as a virgin mother may well have all been based on a misunderstanding of words. Sister Joan Chittister says of that:

> The translation of the word "virgin" itself is in question. Saint Paul, for instance, who writes long before biographical details of Jesus' life began to be inserted into the gospels for the sake of generations to come, explains to the Galatians simply that Jesus was "born of a woman" (Gal 4:4). The original Hebrew text of Isaiah — "a young woman will give birth to Emmanuel" — as quoted in the Gospel of Matthew, does the same. Later translators, however, used the Greek word "parthenos" (virgin) for the Hebrew word "almah" (young woman) because in that culture at that time, a young married woman who had not yet borne a child, scholars now know, could still be called a virgin.[33]

And then there is the biological aspect. As a former Episcopalian bishop has said:

> The moment the world discovered that women had an egg cell which contributed 50% of the genetic code of every new-born life, all virgin birth stories died as literal biology. If Mary is Jesus' mother, and the Holy Spirit the paternal agent, then Jesus would be a half-human, half-divine monster, hardly the claim the church intended. . . . The virgin-birth story was never anything but the stuff of mythology.

Perhaps the church's traditional voices failed to notice that only two of the five major New Testament writers seemed to think it worthy of mention.[34]

The Virgin Birth, a doctrine shared by Catholics, Anglicans and Protestants, was not important at the time when the gospels and epistles that make up our New Testament were being written. It need not be important now. In Catholicism, many other doctrines have gathered around the figure of Mary. There is the Immaculate Conception, declared by Pope Pius IX in 1854 (even though St Thomas Aquinas had disapproved of the idea).[35] There is the Assumption of the Blessed Virgin Mary, which Pope Pius XII declared to be doctrine as recently as 1950.

The Mary of past generations was loved with great devotion, particularly so in Ireland. The more God was portrayed as a severe patriarch, the more the unconditional maternal love was valued in the person of Mary. No matter that the Church taught that she was a model of a sexual purity far beyond the reach of most women, it was her woman's heart that was loved by men and women alike. Now the younger generation is rejecting that image of motherhood without sexuality, and is finding in her a new model of their own. In place of the meek and docile pattern offered by the male Church to its women, Christian women themselves have presented a picture of the strengths and bravery that they saw would have been necessary for all that she went through. She was the woman tough enough to stand up to the shame of unmarried pregnancy, the woman tough enough to stand by the cross of her condemned son. She is also a reminder that, without the involvement of women, the incarnation of God among us is incomplete.

The place of Mary in the divine plan raises a question of major spiritual meaning for the Church: Can the fullness of the vision of God, the totality of the Jesus-message, possibly be achieved even today without the agency of women?

> How real is the birthing of the presence of God among us
> in the churches if women are not involved?[36]

As long as Christianity continues, Mary will continue to be important to us, in various ways according to our various traditions. Many will choose to let go of titles like "Mother of God": but phrases like "Christ-bearer", in which she is seen as an encouragement to all of us to be "Christ-bearers" to others, will continue to be precious.

The Death of Jesus and Its Meaning

At certain times in Christian history, the main spotlight of faith has been on the figure of Jesus being killed by crucifixion. It is a strange but understandable reversal that what might have been a source of shame to his followers at that time became instead a source of pride and glory. If, despite that apparent end to all their hopes, they came through to feeling that he had been so great that his spirit was still with them and that they should continue to follow his teachings and example, then that ignominious ending of his human life would have had to be seen in a new light. Meanings flooded in, all influenced by the Jewish scriptures, or by more primitive ideas of blood-sacrifice. Jesus had been a scapegoat, a creature traditionally sent out into the wilderness to die with the sins of all the people heaped upon it: this was a way for the people to feel their guilt had been lifted off them. Jesus had been the lamb of the atonement: a perfect creature offered to God by slaughter to atone for the sins of the people. The words of the prophet Isaiah were applied to Jesus: he had been "smitten by God", "wounded for our transgressions"; and "upon him was the chastisement that made us whole".[37] Paul, often described as the founder of Christianity although he had never met Jesus, provided the clear explanations. Writing his letters to "the churches" — groups of Christians in various parts of the first-century Mediterranean world — he said "Christ died for our sins, in accordance with the scriptures".[38] All human beings, as descendents of Adam, were sinful and so they would die; but then Jesus had come, and all human beings were "reconciled to God by the death of his Son".[39] As Adam brought death, so Jesus brought life: ". . . as one man's trespass led to condemnation for all, so one man's act of righteousness leads to acquittal and life for all."[40] With time, and especially with the thinking of St Anselm in the eleventh century, the idea developed that God had been so angry with the sinfulness of the people that a blood sacrifice had been necessary. Since humanity had sinned, humanity must pay: only one who was human could offer satisfaction. But, since it was God who was sinned against, only one who was divine could provide it. So the sinless Jesus, of his own free will, had to choose to die to appease the anger of God, and thus save humanity. So said Anselm.

Incredible as it seems, this image of a murderously angry God is still with us. Congregations still cheerfully sing, "He died that we might be forgiven . . . There was no other good enough to pay the price of sin", presumably unaware of the terrible picture of God that lies behind those words. This whole theory of "substitutionary atonement" is summed up in the words "Jesus died for our sins". John Spong has described this theory as now unbelievable.

> Perhaps most troubling of all, the traditional way Christians have told the story of salvation, which focused on the saving act that occurred on the Cross, has become unbelievable to post-modern ears. It is a bizarre concept that turns God into an ogre who requires a blood sacrifice before being able to forgive.[41]

Behind all these rationalisations of his death is the desire to proclaim that Jesus is the saviour of humankind. The emphasis on Jesus' power to save has clearly been a powerful concept throughout Christian history, and must therefore be answering a strong human need. That need proceeds from the sense of sin and guilt that has surely always been a part of human consciousness — or subconsciousness. In varying degrees, we have needed to explain to ourselves the lack of goodness and the failure to be perfect which we see in ourselves and in others. And so, we developed the original sin story of Adam and Eve. Adam, the first man, encouraged by his wife, disobeyed God's instruction not to eat the fruit of the Tree of Knowledge of Good and Evil. Every human being who has existed from that time is said to be a descendant of Adam and Eve, and so have inherited their sinfulness. The biblical story was a simple and symbolic way of saying that the ability to go against goodness, or God, is in us from the start. It was a story that had been told for at least nine centuries before Jesus was born. So when a messiah-figure like Jesus appeared, it would be logical to hope that part of the salvation that he was expected to bring might include salvation from the burden of feeling bad.

How neatly and inevitably it all tied together. Jesus, the charismatic preacher and teacher, is put to death because he is a threat to the secular and religious authorities. Has his mission in life failed? Is it all a disaster? No, his followers jubilantly say, because his spirit is still with us, and so he has proved that there is life after death, and best of all, we can now see that by his death he has reversed the sin of Adam and we have in some miraculous way been freed from all our sins. And look, here are the old scriptural verses which, if you read them correctly, prove that all of this was God's plan from the beginning. For many first-century people, and indeed for vast numbers of the people of the next millennium and a half, or more, this was wonderful news. This was something that gave shape and meaning to their lives and their world. This was powerful. Guilt and sin could be got rid of, and life after death could be attained. On an ever-enlarging structure of observances and rules that would ensure these good things, the Church grew. Spreading the Kingdom of God, which had been all of Jesus' teaching and example, became secondary to being saved from sin and death by Jesus.

Now in the twenty-first century, the concept of "Jesus dying for our sins" has become meaningless to so many Christians, and offensive to so many potential Christians, that it is time to let it become one of the optionals. There are fresh ways of looking at it. The Catholic theologian, Edward Schillebeeckx, offers a positive view of the death of Jesus, as something by which we judge ourselves.

> I . . . no longer see a place for the classical distinction between "God in himself" and "God for us". In the New Testament a theological redefinition of various concepts of God takes place, and also a redefinition of humanity. God accepts humanity without any conditions . . . and precisely through this unconditional acceptance he transforms human beings and brings them to repentance and renewal. Therefore the cross is also a judgement on our autonomous views . . . Here ultimately and definitively is revealed the humanity of God, the heart of Jesus' message of the Kingdom of God . . . so that man and woman become whole and happy, even through suffering.[42]

And here is another angle, from a Scottish ecologist:

> It was precisely this exacting courage, to hold steadfast to God, that Jesus embodied. That is why we cannot ignore him. However, understanding him is not easy. Consider the meaning of the Crucifixion. Traditional Christian theology saw its function as having been to appease, once and for all, God's wrath at human wickedness. This remarkable "doctrine of the atonement" makes out that God was so angry with humankind because of Adam's sin, yet loved His Creation so much, that He sent His son to be the blood sacrifice to appease His own wrath! . . . Well, if that's really how God operates, most folks might be forgiven for thinking that God should get professional help. These ideas derive mainly from Paul, the Church Fathers and later reformers, rather than Jesus' own words in the gospels. They derive from attempts by a patriarchal mindset to interpret tragic events within the constraining framework of

their own worldview dominated by Roman imperialism. Unfortunately, the doctrine of Atonement remains the diet of reactionary fundamentalist preachers. If the metaphorical Devil is watching all this, he must derive very great satisfaction from seeing religion so perverted.

We can, however, look at the Crucifixion in a very different way. It is that Jesus' plight drew a line under the sacrificial religious practices of his culture and time. Jesus, after all, was trying to transform the psyche of humankind, not that of God. . . . He showed that non-violence can cut sharper than the sword. Confronted and refuted by such courage, totalitarian terror could no longer exert its terrible control. Death lost its sting. Life, if we are willing to let it, could be resurrected.[43]

Clare Richards says it in a few words:

. . . basically, the title [Saviour] belongs to God alone (see Luke 1:47 and, strongly, Isaiah 43:11, 45:21). As an image of that saving God, Jesus' ministry is one of rescuing people from their own self-destruction, just like God. And just like all godly people, of course.[44]

The first woman to write a book in the English language had sane things to say about salvation. This fourteenth-century woman recluse, visionary and writer, known as Julian of Norwich, and author of *Revelations of Divine Love*, has gained an enormous following in recent years. A large part of her appeal is the homely and loving picture of Jesus and of God that she portrays, not least in this matter of soteriology, the study of salvation. One of the many books about her says:

Julian of Norwich believes in a God who saves. Belief in a God who saves, belief in a God who draws all human beings to God's self into the eternity of God's loving is a critical concept for a Christian. It is foundational for Christian hope.[45]

Although she considered herself a dutiful daughter of Mother Church, and was sought out by crowds of people for her wisdom and her holiness, Julian was never declared a saint. The most likely reason for that is that some of her views would have been considered heretical at that time. Her famous phrase, "All shall be well, and all shall be well, and all manner of thing shall be well," related to her conviction that all people would be saved. She did not know how that could be, but trusted in God that it would be so. The twentieth-century monk Thomas Merton called her a greater theologian than St Teresa.

If Christianity has a future it lies surely in the letting go of all self-centred salvationism, and uncovering once again the beauty of Jesus' original message of other-centredness. In a simpler Christianity, the death of Jesus will be seen as the natural outcome of his speaking the truth as he saw it, without fear and without compromise. Our salvation lies in following his teachings to whatever end they lead us. In philosophical terms, his death is the triumph of good over evil. It is an archetypal event which we see re-enacted, on a small or large scale, through history and into our own times. It is a death which, like Martin Luther King's and Mahatma Gandhi's and thousands of other "saints", ultimately encourages and enriches the world.

The Resurrection

The most basic fact about life after death is that we cannot know, at least until we die, if it exists. Humanity never has known if it exists, but has always wanted to believe that it does. Most of the world's religions have been built on possible answers to this huge question mark that hangs over our lives. The Jews of Jesus' time were still in dispute over whether there was such a thing as "the resurrection of the body" after death. And then Jesus died, and was buried — "and on the third day he rose again from the dead".[46] And, Paul writes many years later, "he appeared to

Cephas [Peter], then to the twelve. Then he appeared to more than five hundred brethren at one time . . . Then he appeared to James, then to all the apostles. Last of all . . . he appeared also to me."[47]

The gospel accounts are slightly different. In the first-written of the four, the Gospel of Mark, it was to Mary Magdalene that Jesus first appeared, then to "two disciples as they walked", then to "the eleven" (disciples) at table together; and after these appearances Jesus "was received up into heaven and sat on the right hand of God". In the Gospel of Matthew it was to "the women", and then to "the eleven" on a mountain in Galilee. In the Gospel of John it was first to Mary Magdalene, then twice to the disciples gathered together in a locked room, and then to seven of the same disciples on the sea shore. In the Gospel of Luke it was first to two disciples, one called Cleopas, the other unnamed, as they walked the road to Emmaus; then once to "the eleven" in Jerusalem, after which he led them out to Bethany and "was parted from them and carried up into heaven". And in the Acts of the Apostles, written by the same author as "Luke", Jesus presented himself to the (eleven) Apostles, "appearing to them during forty days, and speaking of the Kingdom of God", before being "lifted up . . . out of their sight".

In the past hundred years, many books and articles have been written either to prove that the resurrection of Jesus could and did happen, or to give other explanations for those events.

Joan Chittister says that for most of her young life "the image of Jesus rising from the tomb was just that: Jesus died and came to life again, I thought. And no-one disabused me of the concept. But it troubled me, I must admit, even as a small child." As an adult she came to a more mature conclusion:

> One thing for sure: The Resurrection of Jesus is not about "resuscitation". A corpse does not come to life here and wait again to die. . . . No, the Resurrection of Jesus is not about revivification of an old life, it is about experiencing a new kind of life entirely. And no-one knows how it hap-

pened; we only know that it happened. . . . Resurrection testifies to the metamorphosis of the Jesus of history to the Christ of faith.[48]

But if we proceed under the assumption that whatever happened did not involve an occurrence that broke the laws of nature, and look for a simple and more obvious explanation, then we can say that the most likely reason for these somewhat conflicting accounts is that in the weeks after his death the presence of the spirit of Jesus was sensed by his followers many times and in many different places. Strengthened by this, their "fear of the Jews" fell away until they were emboldened to go out, as we learn in The Acts of the Apostles, and tell the world about Jesus. Whether this change was gradual or dramatically sudden, it must have included an occasion which seemed to them to mark a great turning point. In the second chapter of The Acts of the Apostles we read that on the day of Pentecost a rushing mighty wind and tongues of fire marked the descent of the Holy Spirit of God upon them; after which they were able to speak to people of all nations. Another way of putting it occurs in the Gospel of John, where it is Jesus himself, during one of his appearances to the disciples, who breathes on them and says "Receive the Holy Spirit".[49]

Unfortunately Paul then made, in writing, the large claim that because Jesus "rose from the dead", the resurrection of all people is now proven. In a circular piece of logic, he says:

> Now if Christ is preached as raised from the dead, how can some of you say that there is no resurrection of the dead? But if there is no resurrection of the dead, then Christ has not been raised; if Christ has not been raised, then our preaching is in vain and your faith is in vain. . . . If Christ has not been raised your faith is futile and you are still in your sins.[50]

And so the natural message about the Kingdom of God, which Jesus taught, is turned into a high-pressure message about believing in supernatural events in the life of Jesus and the wonderful effects of believing in them. According to Robert Funk, the founder of the Jesus Seminar in America, this was a deliberate action on the part of the early Church. Belief in the bodily resurrection of Jesus was made a compulsory doctrine to protect the authority of the Church against the gnostic Christians who believed that Jesus appeared not physically but in dreams and visions. The claim of Peter to exclusive leadership was established by his having been the first (apart from some women, that is) to see the risen Christ. If Funk is right, this was not a religious matter, or a theological matter: it was simply a matter of politics.

We are back with the Emperor's invisible clothes. Rationally, we know we can have no proof that Jesus made a bodily resurrection after his own death. Instead, we are told, we must have faith that he did. We can believe the Resurrection, we are told, *if* we believe in Jesus. And we can believe in Jesus because of his resurrection. Alternatively, we can be like the small child who saw that the Emperor had no clothes on and was childlike enough to say so.

What clergy, theologians and others seem increasingly to be saying is that they believe in the resurrection of Jesus, though not necessarily in his *bodily* resurrection. In other words, that he was in some manner experienced again after his death as being with his followers, though not in his original body. Even Paul says, "So it is with the resurrection of the dead . . . It is sown a physical body, it is raised a spiritual body."[51]

The Fellows of the Jesus Seminar are a group of scholars who meet regularly to assess the authenticity of the words and acts of Jesus in the Gospels. They decided to lay their cards on the table regarding this issue. Robert Funk says:

> The Fellows reached a fairly firm consensus: Belief in Jesus'
> resurrection did not depend on what happened to his
> corpse. . . . The empty-tomb story, found in the last chapter
> of the Gospel of Mark, is a late legend, introduced into the
> tradition for the first time by Mark. It was unknown to

Paul. It was also unknown to the Sayings Gospel Q and the Gospel of Thomas.[52] Evidently, the empty-tomb story and the reports of appearances did not come to play a central part in the Jesus tradition until several decades after Jesus' death.[53]

Whatever about the resurrection of Jesus, it is hard to see how so many preachers, and even theologians, jump from the story of Easter day to the assumption that it guarantees life after death for all of us. Tom Wright, the new Bishop of Durham, calls this an error, saying that what the story tells believers is that they belong already, and forever, in the new world "in Christ".[54]

However, to say we have no actual proof of life after death is not to say that there is no such thing. Many of us prefer to say that we simply do not know. Some, influenced by a sense of the continuing presence of those they have loved, think it possible that there is indeed some continuing consciousness beyond our physical life. As to the question of heaven and hell: repeated surveys have shown the numbers of people who believe in a place called hell to be steadily dropping; and the figures for belief in heaven as where you go after death are also declining. Many say that we experience heaven or hell while we are alive, whether through our own actions or through circumstances beyond our control. What this leaves unanswered of course is the question of justice, when those who cause hell for others appear not to be punished, and those who have been through hell in this life appear not to be recompensed. Perhaps, rather than expecting God to do all the work, the heavens and hells of other people are quite simply the responsibility of each one of us, under God.

All we know for sure is that we cannot be sure what happens to us when we die. (And certainly we cannot make statements about the nature of the existence to be experienced after death.) But if our relationship with God is one of confidence and trust then we can cope with not knowing the future. If we are "in" God, then all is well and all manner of thing is well.

The Easter Season

The wonderful season of Easter might appear to be under threat if we revise the meaning of the death of Jesus. Drop the idea of Jesus "paying the price of our sin", of his undergoing a dreadful death in the first century because we in the twenty-first century are being bad, and what does Easter mean? Its original meaning remains and is even stronger for not being saddled with a strange story of an angry God. That meaning — of reassurance that no matter how dark the winter, the resurrection of the earth comes again in spring — surely goes back into the dawn of human life. That there is a connection with our own lives is all the more effective for being stated subtly. "Now the green blade rises from the buried grain", says one of the best of the Easter hymns; ". . . fields of our hearts that dead and bare have been: Love is come again, like wheat that springs up green."[55]

But before Easter comes the season of Lent. How do new-style Christians deal with that? The Lenten ritual, as a time of spiritual stock-taking, is of far greater value than is often realised, and has its spiritual equivalents in all the major world faiths. Lent really deserves a better promotion than the "giving-up-chocolate" routine, which is still surprisingly widespread in Ireland. A time of spring-cleaning or de-toxing of the soul, it can be seen as health-giving rather than flagellatory. And if Good Friday were broadened to include looking not only at the long-ago suffering of Jesus but also at how it is re-enacted in the present suffering of the world, it would be more honest, more accessible and almost certainly more meaningful. Lent can be a time of going down into the dark, looking at what is wrong in our lives; a time of turning in that darkness from self-centredness to other-centredness and coming up into the light by putting into effect, on our own and together, what we thus see needs to be done. Then Easter will dawn for us all with the joy of knowing in our own selves that always out of darkness and death can come light and life.

And what of the event described as the Ascension? Two of the gospels, Mark and Luke, plus the Acts of the Apostles, mention Jesus talking with his disciples, some time after his resurrection, and then being "carried up" or "received up" into heaven. The other two gospels, Matthew and John, make no mention of it. Theologian John Macquarrie dismisses it with the words: "Like the descent [of Jesus after his death] into hell, the ascension cannot be given any historical dimension, for it depends on a mythological conception of the universe." He adds that, as with the resurrection, it is best understood as an event in the disciples, rather than in Jesus.[56] What those passages were saying was that from then on, the Christ was no longer in time and space but was in a new kind of relationship with his followers. In the same book, Macquarrie also talks about the second coming of Christ, expected by his followers. The earliest letters (epistles) of Paul, 1 Thessalonians and 2 Thessalonians, are full of this apparently imminent event. The gospels of Matthew, Mark and Luke, written fifteen and more years later, all contain the words of Jesus, that after times of great tribulation, of false prophets and natural disasters, they would "see the Son of man coming in the clouds of heaven with power and great glory", and that "this generation will not pass away till all these things are fulfilled". It is possible that Jesus was in any case not referring to himself but to some future figure. Whatever about that, in the later epistles Paul has clearly given up that expectation. It fades into the distant future, where it has remained, and has become, as John Macquarrie says, "the source of many superstitions and has led to the growth of many deviant Christian or quasi-Christian sects."[57]

The Logos, the Word of God

"In the beginning was the Word, and the Word was with God, and the Word was God." These beautiful words at the opening of the Gospel of John identify Jesus with the work ("the Word") of God.

That Word is at work at all times and all places, and has been throughout time. One text in the gospels which causes Christians much concern is the assertion of Jesus: "I am the way, the truth, and the life; no one comes to the Father but by me." They are sometimes worried about the fate of non-Christian family members or friends, especially as the sentence is so often used at funerals. Whether those words were actually spoken by Jesus we cannot know. Perhaps they were written in later by the early Church, out of their experience of looking on him as their way, truth and life. Either way, we can be eased by the realisation that the ever-inclusive Jesus, if he spoke those words, would have been identifying himself with the Word (work) of God, saying, in effect, that all who come to God come through the Word/work of God, rather than specifically through the man Jesus. So we need not take it to mean that non-Christians cannot come to God. Nor, on the other hand, do we need to give it the alternative reading that is sometimes suggested: that Buddhists and Hindus and others, if they are in tune with God, are coming to God through Christ without knowing it. It is sufficient to say that all are drawn into God through the Word/work of God, whether through following Jesus or another teacher or guide. It is God who is drawing them, through the way, the truth and the life that is right for them.

Holy Spirit and Trinity

Once the Church declared that Jesus was part of God, they were faced with a dilemma. The Jewish roots of Christianity proclaimed monotheism: God is One. To say that God is One but also somehow Two — Jesus and his Father — is to turn the vastness of God into a one-to-one, face-to-face deity. Numbers were important in the Jewish scriptures. One is one, unique, alone; two is very different and suggests relationship. But to add a third "person" to God, as the early Church did formally in the Nicene Creed in 325 AD ("*And we believe also in One Holy Spirit*") is to turn those

figures into a suggestion of infinity. Just as the number four traditionally suggested the solidity of the earth, and three the limitlessness of the heavens, so the doctrine of the Trinity, "three
persons in one God", suggested the limitlessness of God.

But that was then, and this is now, and our twenty-first century minds work differently. Stephen Platten (now Bishop of
Wakefield) and George Pattison wrote in a recent essay: "Essential
trinitarianism in the sense meant by the early Church Fathers may
now be an irrecoverable concept."[58] The Catholic theologian Karl
Rahner has said that to talk of the fatherhood and sonhood of God
is to be economical with the truth.[59] The trouble is that when only
a minority of the population have any real theological education,
phrases such as "three persons in one God" reduce the greatness
of God to human proportions. What we call the Old Testament
says that we must not make images of God, and there is great
wisdom in this. To paint a picture of God or make a sculpture of
God is, like making many statements about God, a form of trying
to control God. It is misguiding because it damages our sense of
what God is. God is no longer greater than anything we can imagine but is, in our heads, that painting by Michelangelo or Blake, or
that medieval sculpted relief we saw once in a church or cathedral. It is very human of us to want to have such pictures in our
head. But it limits the wonder and the glory of God to a human-
sized shape. Indeed, many Christians, when they use the word
"God", are in actual fact concentrating on Jesus, so that the image
of God they carry in their heads and hearts is only a human-
shaped God.

If we let go of the idea of Jesus being the "second person" in
God, what do we do with the concept of the Holy Spirit? In practice the "third person" has always been rather vague and amor-
phous. Through the centuries, the popular emphasis on different
aspects of God has swung like a pendulum. Sometimes God the
Father was the popular one, sometimes Jesus the Christ. In the
dark times of the early Middle Ages, the focus was on Jesus as the

one who would judge humankind at the end of the world. In the later Middle Ages it was on Jesus and his suffering and crucifixion. In the nineteenth century, in the British Empire at least, it seems to have been on God the Father Almighty, omnipotent, majestic and all-knowing; a sort of larger version of Victoria, Queen and Empress. In the twentieth century, following two world wars, the pendulum swung back to Jesus, but this time to the loving, caring Jesus surrounded by little sheep and small children. But this pendulum swinging always ignored the Third Person. Then in the final decades of the twentieth century that changed. The forgotten figure of the Holy Spirit burst into our churches, causing people to "speak in tongues" and later to be "slain in the Spirit". Even in the non-charismatic churches it was rare for any sort of meeting not to make some reference to the guiding of the Holy Spirit. Recognising the increased pace of the pendulum, which in one century had covered all three "persons" of the Trinity, many of us at that time began to wonder where it would go next.

Now we see the answer: now the emphasis is turning to God *as* God, God-in-Godself. God is One. To talk of Jesus as part of God is not to say that one particular human being was uniquely part of God but rather that in and through Jesus we saw that *all* human life is in God. To talk of the Holy Spirit is not to talk of a ghostly person who is also tucked up there in God but a way of talking of the power of God, God's spirit, moving among us. There is no need to posit a separate "person". The Holy Spirit is in no way different from "God", because God *is* Spirit. "The Spirit is not other than God himself," the Catholic theologian Hans Küng has said.

> "Spirit" as understood in the Bible means — as opposed to "flesh", to created, perishable reality — *the force or power proceeding from God*: that invisible force of God and power of God that is effective, creatively or destructively, for life or judgement, in creation and history, in Israel and later in the Church. . . . The Spirit is *not other than God himself*. He is

God himself close to man and the world, as the compre-
hending but not comprehensible, the bestowing but not
controllable, the life-creating but also judging, power and
force. This is important. The Holy Spirit is not a third party,
not a thing between God and men, but God's personal
closeness to men.[60]

Those words were published twenty-five years ago. Serious theologians have been saying this sort of thing for some time.

For [M.F.] Wiles, as for [G.W.H.] Lampe, the trinitarian
model was in the end less satisfactory for the articulation of
basic Christian experience than the unifying concept of God
as Spirit. For Wiles, it is of particular importance to stress
that trinitarian orthodoxy simply claims too much knowledge of God.[61]

Does all this mean we have to lose the lovely word Trinity? Even
if the words of our prayers and our liturgy are gradually altered,
many churches and cathedrals are named after the Trinity. But
there is another way of looking at that phrase. The concept of
Trinity still has value if we can reclaim it as the ancient tradition
of putting words together in threes when talking of God, such as
"Being, Increasing, Fulfilment", or "Creator, Redeemer, Sus-
tainer", and in this way proclaiming that through the practice of
"three-in-one-ness" God can be expressed and experienced in a
multitude of ways. Adrian B. Smith writes:

Today theologians are proposing other expressions to give
a contemporary meaning to our belief in a triune God. For
example, thinking of God as Being (not as "a" being nor
even as "the" being) John Macquarrie proposes "move-
ments" or "modes" of Being. The Father may be thought of
as "primordial" Being, the Son as "expressive" Being, the
Spirit as "unitive" Being. Others propose that the Biblical
Father, Son and Spirit can be understood as different
modes of God's action — Knowing, Serving and Loving —
or as three distinguishable ways in which the one God is

experienced as acting in relation to us: as Creator, as Redeemer, as Inspirer. . . . What is common to all these expressions is that in the Godhead there is both unity and
diversity.[62]

The American theologian Norman Pittenger sees the triune God
as being God above us ("transcendent"), and God with us ("con-
comitant"), and God in us ("immanent"). All of these seem to be
saying that God is multi-faceted, like a cut diamond, throwing
light in many different directions. It reminds us that God can be
discovered in hundreds of different ways and in thousands of different guises. Dr Martyn Percy says: "Ultimately, all the doctrine
of the Trinity is trying to do is to say something about the abun-
dance of God."[63] I have over my desk a reproduction of the famous Rublev icon, in which three long-robed androgynous
figures represent the men/angels who visited Abraham, but also
the Trinity. The freedom it gives, to see or not see specific images
and situations, in various times and places, is wonderfully creative. It provides the very spaces in between our hard-edged
knowledge in which almost by chance we discover in unplanned
moments the reality of God.

We Christians have always claimed to be monotheists. But that
claim has been compromised by fourth- and fifth-century theology, which went through such intellectual contortions to get Jesus
included in God. In 1553, Michael Servetus, a country doctor with
a reputation for selflessness in the care of his patients, published a
book declaring that the doctrine of the Trinity was not mentioned
in the Bible, was not known in heaven, and was a nonsensical
invention of the Council of Nicaea. When he was burned at the
stake for heresy, a copy of the book was chained to his body to
burn with him.[64] There have been others who have rejected
trinitarianism: Unitarianism has a long and honourable history. It
has taken many centuries, but now at last even mainline Christians
are beginning to be able to say with integrity that we believe in
One God.

If we do really believe that the God of Judaism, and the God of Islam, is the same God as the God of Christianity — and few Christians now would deny that — then we must surely assume that what that universal God has revealed to the Jews and the Muslims is as valid and authentic as that which has been revealed to Christians. Not necessarily the same, but valid and authentic. This will be difficult for us to grasp if we have been brought up to think that there is one absolute truth, and we just happen to be the lucky ones who have it. Maybe there is such a thing as absolute truth: but if so, it is far, far bigger than any one human brain — or any one culture — can command. In this our one human life, we can only expect to comprehend small areas of it. Few have said this better than Rabbi Jonathan Sacks in his book *The Dignity of Difference*.

> The radical transcendence of God in the Hebrew Bible means nothing more or less than that there is a difference between God and religion. God is universal, religions are particular. Religion is the translation of God into a particular language and thus into the life of a group, a nation, a community of faith. In the course of history, God has spoken to mankind in many languages: through Judaism to Jews, Christianity to Christians, Islam to Muslims. Only such a God is truly transcendental — greater not only than the natural universe but also than the spiritual universe articulated in any single faith, any specific language of human sensibility. How could a sacred text convey such an idea? It would declare that *God is God of all humanity, but no single faith is or should be the faith of all humanity*. Only such a narrative would lead us to see the presence of God in people of other faiths. Only such a worldview could reconcile the particularity of cultures with the universality of the human condition.[65]

Such a view, by people of all faiths, is surely the only hope for the future of religion and of the world.

Muslims and Jews and Christians, with their common roots and shared history, are sometimes called "the people of the book": the Torah, the Bible, the Qur'an. If the God of the people of the book is the same one God, can we look wider still? Can we ask, for example, if the "God" of Hindus and Buddhists is the same one God? The God of the Hindus is like the Christian Trinity carried to an extreme: God is expressed in hundreds of different forms and different ways. For Buddhists, God is so all-pervasive that they do not use the word "God". Yet surely, if there is a God at all, that God must be the same one God of all. This is a very liberating thought. Once we accept that our God is God to *all* peoples, we are set free from thinking that the concepts and ideas which our own particular culture have given us are fixed forever. If they are good, if they are helpful, then let us retain them. But if they are actually damaging us as persons, or damaging our faith community, then it must be right to let them go. The image of a wrathful, punishing God has ruined many lives even to the point of suicide. The idea of a kill-joy God has made life close to being hell on earth for many communities in the past. The requirement to believe in miraculous births or bodily resurrections or any other of what *Alice in Wonderland* called "six impossible things before breakfast" is even now causing the slow death of many congregations. None of these death-dealing things fit with the teaching of Jesus, the man of godly love whom we claim to follow. We must be able to let them go.

Notes

---

[1] E.J. Tinsley, in *A New Dictionary of Christian Theology*, ed. A. Richardson & J. Bowden (SCM Press, 1983).

[2] F.C. Happold, *Mysticism* (Penguin, 1963).

[3] Paul Tillich, *The Shaking of the Foundations* (Penguin, 1949).

[4] Joan Chittister OSB, *In Search of Belief* (Redemptorist Publications, 1999).

[5] Paragraph 213 of *The Catechism of the Catholic Church* (Geoffrey Chapman, London, 1994).

[6] Liturgy of St John Chrysostom, Anaphora.

[7] Paragraphs 40, 42, of *The Catechism of the Catholic Church* (Geoffrey Chapman, London, 1994).

[8] Giles Fraser, "Telling the people in the pews that God isn't a thing", in *The Church Times*, 14 March 2003.

[9] Dan Cohn-Sherbok, "A mystery beyond our conception", in *The Church Times*, 25 January 2002.   *See p. 58*

[10] Richard Dawkins, *A Devil's Chaplain* (Weidenfeld & Nicholson, 2003).

[11] Dietrich Bonhoeffer, *Letters and Papers from Prison* (SCM Press, 1953).

[12] Don Cupitt, *The Sea of Faith* (BBC, 1984).

[13] Adrian B. Smith, *A New Framework for Christian Belief* (CANA, 2001).

[14] Paul Tillich, *The Shaking of the Foundations* (Penguin, 1949).

[15] Denys Turner, *The Darkness of God: Negativity in Christian Mysticism* (Cambridge University Press, 1995).

[16] Julian of Norwich, *Revelations of Divine Love*, trans. Clifton Wolters (Penguin, 1966).

[17] Inayat Bunglawala, "Face to Faith", in *The Guardian*, 3 February 2003.

[18] John Hick, *The Fifth Dimension* (Oneworld, 1999).

[19] R.P.C. Hanson, "The unexamined assumption of most Christian believers", in *The Times*, 10 June 1978.

[20] Clare Richards, *Introducing Catholic Theology* (Kevin Mayhew, 2002).

[21] Adrian B. Smith, *A New Framework for Christian Belief* (CANA, 2001*)*.

[22] This was said by William Temple, later to become Archbishop of Canterbury.

[23] Hugh Montefiore, *Credible Christianity* (Mowbray, 1993).

[24] Hugh Montefiore, *Looking Afresh: Soundings in Creative Dissent* (SPCK, 2003).

[25] John Macquarrie, *Jesus Christ in Modern Thought* (SCM Press, 1990).

[26] Hugh Montefiore, *Credible Christianity* (Mowbray, 1993).

[27] Joan Chittister, OSB, *In Search of Belief* (Redemptorist Publications, 1999).

[28] Norman Pittenger, *Christology Reconsidered* (SCM Press, 1970).

[29] Frances Young, in *The Myth of God Incarnate*, edited by John Hick (SCM Press, 1977).

[30] John Shelby Spong, *Why Christianity Must Change or Die* (Harper Collins, NY, 1998).

[31] Pages 30 and 4, in *The Myth of God Incarnate*, edited by John Hick (SCM Press, 1977).

[32] John Macquarrie, *Jesus Christ in Modern Thought* (SCM Press, 1990).

[33] Joan Chittister, OSB, *In Search of Belief* (Redemptorist Publications, 1999).

[34] Jack Spong, "The church is dead, long live the reformation", in *The Guardian*, 9 December 2000.

[35] See p. 210 of *Papal Sin,* by Garry Wills (Doubleday, 2000).

[36] Joan Chittister, OSB, *In Search of Belief* (Redemptorist Publications, 1999).

[37] The Book of Isaiah 53:4,5.

[38] First Epistle to the Corinthians 15:3.

[39] Epistle to the Romans 5:10.

[40] Epistle to the Romans 5:18.

[41] Jack Spong, "The church is dead, long live the reformation", in *The Guardian*, 9 December 2000.

[42] E. Schillebeeckx, *Jesus in our Western Culture* (SCM, 1987).

[43] Alistair McIntosh, *Soil and Soul* (Aurum, 2001).

[44] Clare Richards, *Introducing Catholic Theology* (Kevin Mayhew, 2002).

[45] Kerrie Hide, *Gifted Origins to Graced Fulfilment: the Soteriology of Julian of Norwich* (Liturgical Press, 2001).

[46] The Apostles' Creed.

[47] First Epistle to the Corinthians 15:5–8.

[48] Joan Chittister, OSB, *In Search of Belief* (Redemptorist Publications, 1999).

[49] John 20:22.

[50] First Epistle to the Corinthians 15:12–17.

[51] First Epistle to the Corinthians 15:42, 44.

[52] These are two of several early gospels which were not included in the "official" Bible.

53 Robert W. Funk, *Honest to Jesus* (Harper, San Francisco, 1996).

54 N.T. Wright, *The Resurrection of the Son of God* (SPCK, 2003).

55 Hymn 278, *Church Hymnal* (OUP, 2000).

56 John Macquarrie, *Jesus Christ in Modern Thought* (SCM Press, 1990).

57 John Macquarrie, *Jesus Christ in Modern Thought* (SCM Press, 1990).

58 Stephen Platten and George Pattinson, *Spirit and Tradition: an Essay on Change* (Canterbury Press, 1996).

59 Karl Rahner, *The Trinity*, trans. J. Donceel (Herder & Herder, 1970).

60 Hans Küng, *Does God Exist?* (William Collins & Sons Ltd, 1978).

61 David F. Ford, *The Modern Theologians* (Blackwell, 1997).

62 Adrian B. Smith, *A New Framework for Christian Belief* (CANA, 2001).

63 Martyn Percy, "Reloading the Trinity" in *The Guardian, 14 June 2003.*

64 Lawrence and Nancy Goldstone, *Out of the Flames* (Century, 2003).

65 Jonathan Sacks, *The Dignity of Difference* (Continuum, 2002).

Chapter 5

FEEDING THE SOUL

"Good faith, in my view, is about throwing things away all
the time, not holding on to unjustifiable premises"
— *Bishop Richard Holloway*

Reading the Bible

There is quite a wide range of opinions about how true the Bible is. The most fundamental is the idea that it was written personally by God, or dictated word for word to Moses and other prophets of the Hebrew scriptures, and to Matthew, Mark, Luke and John of the Christian (New) Testament. People may move from that position to saying instead that all the writings were inspired by God. But there they may stick, with the belief that since they were inspired every word is to be believed and acted upon. (The difficulties arise when they are asked whether they think they should now be killed for eating shellfish, or cooking meat and dairy products together, or wearing clothes of two fibres mixed together — such as polycotton shirts, all of which are forbidden in the scriptures.) Another view would be that the various books of the Bible were written by human beings with a special interest in explaining the ways of God to their fellow human beings, and who did their best to write what they truthfully believed. Others might bring in the effects of time and of ecclesiastical politics on the way these documents have been handed down to us, with changes being made here and there, pieces added or subtracted, and translations from the original languages causing errors. "A virgin shall conceive and bring forth a child" (Isaiah 7:14) is a well-known example of this sort of misunderstanding, where the word "virgin", as we saw in Chapter 4, is now known simply to have meant a young woman. More and more people are becoming aware that something which had a particular meaning two or more millennia ago — the word "leprosy" for example, or "possession by devils" — may not have exactly the same meaning now when our medical knowledge is more advanced.

These are, in a sense, all practical concerns to do with facts. A broader shift of understanding is called for when we look at how the overall meaning was heard at the time of writing, and whether we hear it differently now. Take the story of Jonah and the whale. Did a man really live inside a large sea creature for several days? Did people ever think that was literally possible? Well, a few gullible people may have, as did many of us when we were very young. Yet we don't need to ask: Is it real? The story is a parable, a vivid way for the writer to picture what he felt God was saying at that time. Then there is, in the story of Jesus, the account of that journey into Egypt made by Joseph and Mary with the infant Jesus, to escape Herod's jealous rampage of murder of all the children under two years of age in and around Bethlehem. This journey is mentioned only in Matthew's Gospel. If such a fearful journey literally happened, would we not expect it to occur in the other gospels as well? Or is it just a way of saying something else? Matthew's account ends with words "that it might be fulfilled which was spoken of the Lord by the prophet, saying, 'Out of Egypt have I called my son'".[1] By that reference perhaps he was saying that the newborn Jesus was "Israel" and was in some way representing all the Jewish people.

Was there really an Adam and Eve? If they were the beginning of the human race, how could their sons and daughters produce more children without engaging in incest? Trying to apply reason to Bible stories, says Christian ecologist Alistair McIntosh, is like "trying to explain a space rocket through scientific principles contained in the Psalms". The Western mind, he says, has not realised it has been using the wrong tools, with the result that myth has become incredible instead of being seen as a reference frame. "Bereft of poetic knowing and the emotional engagement of feeling, the rich and warm metaphorical meanings that can be discerned in the Holy Scriptures and other sources of wise story have withered".[2]

Do we read the Scriptures mytho-poetically or rationally? The reason we have reached a crisis point now is that, although we have continued to read the Bible, we have been reading myth and poetics far too literally. And unless we have studied theology or literature at university level, or are receiving particularly good adult religious education, or are just exceptionally well read, that is what our modern minds assume we must do. We think: "The Bible says angels appeared, so: angels must have appeared." We are not taught to think: "The Bible says angels appeared, so from that we can understand that the presence of God was felt in that situation, and was described as the presence of angels." Christian thinking has its roots in Greek rationalism *and* in Hebrew poetics, and somewhere along the line we have swung too heavily into the rational side. This has happened not just in our religion but in European culture generally. From time to time, there have been surges of counterbalancing, especially in the arts. A few examples would be surrealism, impressionism, dadaism, futurism, cubism, theatre of the absurd, and Artaud's theatre of cruelty (a specific aim of which was to overthrow the theatre of rationality). In religion, the rebellion against a literal reading of the scriptures is a similar counterbalancing. Science, which for a long time had been seen as the enemy of religion, is now more often an ally, with both being said to be "irreducibly metaphorical". This would be the viewpoint of John Habgood, who until recently was Archbishop of York, and is both scientist and cleric. He says: "In every narrative there is that which is not said, and cannot be said, but can only be glimpsed out of the corner of an eye."

A much more intuitive way of reading scripture is gaining ground with the newly popularised practice of *lectio divina*. Coming from Benedictine roots, this is the slow reading of a chosen passage from the Bible, each person allowing any particular phrase to demand their attention. In the following silence they are invited to realise why that passage has significance for them and, subsequently, what action it might call for in their lives. As the American writer Norvene Vest explains:

> In *lectio* we read not to receive information, for basically we already know what the Bible says. We read to interact with the Word of God; we read to respond to what God offers our life this day.[3]

Michel de Verteuil, a Spiritan priest, claims that *lectio divina* is the most important part of "community theology", or monastic theology, which prevailed for the first millennium of Christianity before it was overtaken by academic ("school") theology. "The Church will always need school theology," he says, "but it must be complemented by community theology."[4]

It would be a mistake to think of any of the books of the New Testament as untouched after their original writing-down. Some of the Gospel words of Jesus we have to discount as all too obviously having been added by following generations. For example, "Go ye therefore and teach all nations, baptising them in the name of the Father, and of the Son, and of the Holy Ghost" (Matthew 28:19) could hardly have been said by Jesus, as the concept of the Trinity had not yet been developed. The words of Jesus in the Gospel of John are so different from those in the other three Gospels that, as we have seen, it is widely assumed that John's work is more a theology of Jesus than any sort of biography. Full of poetry and deeply spiritual it is; straight history it is not.

The Hebrew scriptures, which Christians have long called the Old Testament, are relatively new to Roman Catholics. In Ireland, it is commonly said that they were not allowed read them until fairly recently, although some of the basic stories, like Noah's Ark, and Adam and Eve, were told. This is not in fact true: Catholics were never forbidden to read the Old Testament. They were, however, forbidden to read Protestant translations of the Bible on the grounds that these were often slanted in favour of Protestant doctrinal positions. The Catholic translations were based on the Latin Vulgate. Likewise, Protestants did not read Catholic translations for similar reasons.[5] Now that all our churches read all the main parts of the Bible in church, normally in a three-year cycle, the riches of many of the older books are being fully appreciated. There was for a long time a tradition of valuing the Old Testament mostly for what were seen, looking backwards, as prophecies of the coming of the Christ. That trend is weakening now, and the writings of the prophets and the books of wisdom and the early stories of the Jewish people are allowed stand in their own right, part of the history of the development of the relationship of those people with God. As such, they do not have nearly as much influence on Christian doctrine as the New Testament does.

Miracles

In any Bible study group, the subject of miracles is a great discussion charger. Did they really happen? Did the Red Sea really part to let the Israelites through to safety? Did Jesus really walk on the water? Were five loaves and two fishes really turned into enough food to feed the vast crowd listening to Jesus in the desert? Why do miracles not happen now? Or do they? None of these questions are answered in the Catholic Catechism, which takes it for granted that miracles occur. It merely says that they are "oriented towards sanctifying grace, and are intended for the common good of the Church". The miracles of Jesus "strengthen faith in the One who does his Father's works". But it adds that they are "not intended to satisfy people's curiosity or desire for magic".[6] The standard dictionary definition of the word "miracle" is that it is an event exceeding or contrary to the known powers of nature, and therefore thought to be due to the special intervention of the Deity or of some supernatural agency.

"Contrary to the *known* powers of nature": there is the core of the matter. As the workings of nature were gradually learned by humanity, the number of "miracles" have dropped proportionately. These days we reserve the word for something that is merely against the odds — but especially where prayer has been involved — as with someone recovering unexpectedly from cancer; or finding a desperately needed parking place in a crowded city. Miracles reflect their times: the ones recorded in the Bible are not very different from accounts of miracles in other cultures of those periods. In the Middle Ages, miracles were regarded as essential proof that Christian revelation was divinely inspired. (This attitude survives in the sort of argument where a Christian will say, for example, that we know God wrote the Bible because it says in the Bible that God wrote the Bible.) In the eighteenth century, philosophy and physics spelt the end of widespread belief in miracles, and the beginning of naturalistic explanations, such as the idea that the crowd gathered for the Sermon on the Mount had actually all brought some food with them and were shamed by Jesus into producing it and sharing it. Twentieth-century theologians have tended to focus on what the gospel writers were actually trying to convey when they recorded miraculous events. Sociologists, on the other hand, have looked at the social function of belief in miracles. Miracle stories about a holy person are testimonies to society's regard for that person; personal experience of miracle can bolster an individual's sense of being cared for by God, thereby producing gratitude and devotion; but "claims to perform miracles belong to the sphere of manipulation of power".[7]

The whole question of miracles is very much a "God of the gaps" area. But prayed-for things do indeed happen when the odds are stacked sky-high against them, and we may yet find that it is a fact that the focused energies of people can change events.

However implausible the Gospel stories of the miracles wrought by Jesus may be, they all point in one direction. Love heals. In some degree, after contact with him blind people could see, deaf people could hear, lame people could walk. In this man, godly love combined with trust and the detachment of selflessness caused great things to happen. We will never know the details. On the other hand, we do have a record of a large number of his sayings and teachings. On these alone it would be possible to fix a claim to be a Christian, that is, a follower of Jesus, the Christ, the "anointed one". His teachings are perfections mostly above our reach but rarely beyond our attempting. They are a blueprint for the domain ("Kingdom") of God, a world allowed to be filled with God.

Sacraments and Worship

In a simplified, less-structured Christianity we might expect to have a simpler approach to the idea of sacraments than the Church currently gives. The rigidity of the present situation is epitomised in the fact that there are differing views on the number of sacraments that exist. In the Roman Catholic Church the answer to "How many sacraments are there?" is "Seven: baptism, confirmation, Eucharist, penance, the anointing of the sick, holy orders and matrimony." In the Anglican Church (e.g. the Church of Ireland) they normally answer something like this: "Christ in the Gospel has appointed two sacraments for his Church, as needed by all for fullness of life, baptism and holy communion", adding "Other sacramental ministries of grace are confirmation, ordination, holy matrimony, the ministry of absolution, and the ministry of healing." The difference between the two and the seven lies only in the question as to whether or not Jesus instituted them in his lifetime. He is said to have instituted holy communion by blessing bread and wine at his final supper with his disciples and saying words such as "This is my body" and "This is my blood" and "Do this in remembrance of me". He is said to have instituted baptism by his command recorded in Matthew 28, quoted above. Arguably, he also absolved people of their sins ("Go, your sins are forgiven") and healed people (though not, as far as we know, by anointing them). There is no record of his confirming as such, or ordaining or marrying.

A sacrament is "the use of material things as signs and pledges of God's grace, and as a means by which we receive his gifts". It is "an outward and visible sign of inward and spiritual grace".

Why then are sacraments restricted to a list of seven, or two, or indeed any number? Increasingly now, Christians are seeing sacraments in any material thing that lets in, or shows forth, the presence of the divine in our midst. A flower in the hedgerow, a communal meal, the giving of an engagement ring, even a child sharing its toys with another. One effect of the concept being broadened in this way is that it passes beyond the control of ecclesiastical authority into the hands of ordinary people. We do not need an ordained person to stage-manage any of the above examples. The divine can be seen and felt in the flower, the meal, the ring, the toys, as long as those present can see and feel it. That is all it takes. All of life is sacramental to those who can see it, feel it. Such a way of looking at the word "sacrament" is valuable, since Christians such as Quakers and the Salvation Army do not have formal sacraments, but often find this description very acceptable.

Yet many of us will still want to have formal sacramental rituals as well, and for these it is good to have, as we do now, people who are trained or skilled in leading them. There are two issues here: experience and spirituality. Although they are presumed to be both present in ordained ministry, this is not always so. As a Christian priest, I have more than once been asked by friends to conduct non-religious funeral services — because they knew I knew how to do a funeral service, and the family could relax. That is the experience side of ministry. When those who conduct the sacramental services are also God-centred people, it is a tremendous bonus, enabling the congregation to be caught up in an awareness of the presence of the divine. Unfortunately, due to current pressures to select and train and place sufficient numbers of clergy, we do not always have this. It may be that social and practical pressures will force some quite large rethinking of ministry. Many Catholics have expressed the view that God may be speaking through the shortage of ordinands and the clergy's loss of status after the many revelations of sexual abuse, and that the result will be married priests and women priests. A subsequent result would be the removal of all those unhealthy priestly pedestals. Garry Wills makes the interesting point that when all other reasons for celibacy were found to be inadequate, what was retained was the argument that an unmarried priest would be more "available", but that in fact all it produced was a clergy distanced by difference. He also says that the wearing of ornate vestments marks the priest as standing apart from others, while the required daily reading of the breviary provides a further withdrawal, and that all this heightens the priest's "monopolistic control of [the] sacred transaction" of the Eucharist.[8] There is much here that will be changed in the years ahead, perhaps building on the work of Liberation Theology and experiments such as that of the "worker priests". Indeed, the larger result of the need for changes in ministry may be a rethinking of the concept of priesthood altogether, and this would have influence in the other Christian churches as well as among Catholics. The practice of ordination does not go back to Jesus' time: there were no Christian priests until at least forty years after his death.

For vast numbers of Christians, the Eucharist, or service of Holy Communion, is the centre of their religious practice. What it actually signifies varies from denomination to denomination. Even within a denomination, its meaning will in practice differ from one individual to another. At one extreme it is simply a remembrance of the last supper Jesus had with his disciples. At the other extreme, the bread and the wine become the very body and blood of Christ. The doctrine which describes this change is known in the Catholic Church as transubstantiation; it has caused huge problems through the ages and still does for many people. Most Catholics think that most Protestants do not believe in it, which is true; but they are on the whole unaware that most Anglicans (Church of Ireland, Church of England, Episcopalians, etc.) are happy to proclaim what is known as the Real Presence: that Jesus is in some indefinable way present in the bread and wine that is consecrated and shared at a service of Holy Communion. This is reasonably close to transubstantiation, though without *necessarily* including an insistence on a literal, physical understanding of the word "presence".

This issue was clarified by ARCIC (the Anglican and Roman Catholic International Commission). Their Final Report was published in 1982, summing up more than a decade's work that had begun in 1966 with a Common Declaration by Pope Paul VI and Archbishop Michael Ramsey of the Anglican Church, although sadly the document is now considered as having little authority. On the subject of the presence of Christ in the Eucharist, the Report talks about the Real Presence — and it is a shame that its words are not better known by the people in all our pews:

> Criticism has been evoked by the [earlier] statement that the bread and wine become the body and blood of Christ in the eucharist. . . . The word *become* has been suspected of expressing a materialistic conception of Christ's presence, and this has seemed to some to be confirmed in the footnote on the word *transubstantiation* which also speaks of change. It is feared that this suggests that Christ's presence in the eucharist is confined to the elements, and that the Real Presence involves a physical change in them. . . . *Becoming* does not here imply material change. Nor does the liturgical use of the word imply that the bread and wine become Christ's body and blood in such a way that in the eucharistic celebration his presence is limited to the consecrated elements. It does not imply that Christ becomes pre-

sent in the eucharist in the same manner that he was present in his earthly life. . . . The bread and wine *become* the
sacramental body and blood of Christ in order that the
Christian community may *become* more truly what it already is, the body of Christ.[9]

The common belief of Roman Catholics that all Protestants —
in which they include Anglicans — only think of Holy Communion as a memorial, or remembrance, is quite inadequate. On the
other hand, there are numbers of Church of Ireland people, especially in the North of Ireland for example, who would be against
even the use of the phrase "Real Presence". And there are apparently growing numbers of Catholics (up to 38 per cent in America)[10] who would not be willing to say that the body and blood of
Christ is literally present in the bread and wine of the Eucharist.
This whole issue is vitally important, and is one on which a common view for millions could surely be found.

Yet no matter how varied our thinking on this may be, the actual ritual is still powerful and potentially health-giving for themselves and the community of which they are a part. That need not
change. Everywhere now people are taking it into their own
hands to have private "Eucharistic" gatherings, with or without
ordained clergy and with or without the approved liturgy, the
approved sets of words. Clearly this could be seen by the Church
as dangerous stuff, and the official line is to forbid it. Nevertheless, it will certainly go on and increase, at least until all hope of
future life for Christianity has died. Some of these gatherings are
very basic: people sitting around a table, taking bread and wine
into their hands with the reverence due to all life-sustaining food,
and by saying the name of Jesus connecting to his life and his
spirit, and then continuing with a communal meal. Others are
more formal, but again usually innovative in some way or another. It is possible, for example, to share almost an entire Eucharist in silence if plans are made beforehand for certain parts such
as "the repentance" and "the thanksgiving" to be indicated by ac-

tions, so that everyone is taking part interiorly. In most of these, the role of the celebrant is usually less dominant than in the traditional forms, and this probably reflects the fact that generally it is women who are involved.

If the Church is to continue, and if the celebration of the Eucharist is to continue, we will be influenced by these experimental forms. There has been a lot of recent liturgical revision, yet it is perhaps too little and too late. A rebirth of images is desperately needed to satisfy the spiritual hunger of our times, says the scientist Arthur Peacocke.[11] The old ways can surely continue as long as they are valued, but the main offering of a church in the community will be services of worship that involve the right side of the brain as well as the left: that can be experienced rather than simply heard. We will let go of the endless pages of words, and fine them down to a few regulars, like the "Our Father", the Lord's Prayer, which almost anyone of any Christian faith can say with integrity, and one or two brief readings from ancient and modern sources. There will be art or music, any that allow us glimpses of the divine; with singing, and times of reflection, and times of sacramental action like the holding or washing of each other's hands, and the blessing and breaking and sharing of bread.

With the exception of the Eucharist and absolution, the Church's sacraments as they now exist are rites of passage. A child enters the world, or two people leave singleness and become a couple, or a man or woman becomes a spiritual leader of some sort. Confirmation is arguably a rite of passage from childhood to adulthood, though with changes in the age at which it is administered it rarely functions as such. In recent decades, a great deal of time and effort by liturgical committees has gone into rewriting the words for many of these "rite-of-passage" services, but they have been mere tinkerings, compared with what will be needed. It is no new thing to say that people are beginning to ask for other rites as well. Already in the Anglican Church there exists a form of "Thanksgiving for the Birth of a Child", which came into being through so many parents expressing unease with the concept of baptism, or unreadiness for it. Already some Church bodies are thinking about running into one the rites of baptism and confirmation and the first reception of holy communion, so that children (or adults) would be full members of the Church from the time of their baptism, as in the Orthodox Church. New ways will need to be found for those rites which are retained, ways that are less wordy and more to do with experiencing, through material and sensual things like water, fire, plants, circles, hands, breath. These are the things that make a rite truly "sacramental"; an overload of words with one meagre material symbol cannot. It is because the rites of the Church have become so dry, so left-brain led, that numbers of people are turning instead to things like circle dancing, T'ai Chi, and spiritual forms of yoga, where the body as well as the head is involved. This is the basis of sacrament.

Further rites will need to be devised for other times of passage. The blessing of friendships, the release of the other at the end of a relationship, various forms of forgiveness, various rites of healing, the blessing of a family or other group in which there is someone with a terminal illness, blessings on journeys and ventures and failures, thanksgivings for achievements: all of these are needed, and most of them are already being provided here and there by people who want them. Such rites may be ephemeral, created for a specific occasion and specific people, or they may be published and circulated so that what one group has found good others may benefit from. In the past, this would have been seen as dangerous by those who have sought to keep liturgical creativity within their own very tight control. But those days are passing. If new ways are resisted, then the machinery of control will simply be left high and dry with the deep waters of change swirling on by.

Other forms of worship will also need to become more right-brain if they are to commend themselves. Ideally and basically, worship would be seen as a continuous process, from waking to sleeping, through every day of the week.

Prayer

At present, many Christians still say at least a quick prayer on awaking and another before going to sleep; most, I suspect, would not even expect that much of themselves. The attitude of many church-going, Mass-going Christians is that on the whole the clergy are paid to pray for them: *they* can do the daily praying, and once a week into the church building will do for the non-professionals. It feels like a freedom, the not-having-to, but in actuality it is self-starvation. Without knowing it, people are starving themselves. When participation in worship becomes a once-a-week duty to God or the neighbours or the Inner Parent, then it is dry and unpalatable, and cannot be absorbed. Sunday or sabbath worship is a tradition going back to the time of Moses, and originated with the wise perception that human beings needed a regular time of rest, a regular day that was different from other days. In the best-known version of the Ten Commandments, God is believed to have told Moses' people to remember to "keep holy" the seventh day of the week. Through the centuries, this injunction hardened into the concept that once in every seven days you should go into a communal building and together go through a certain form of words and actions that would be a communication with God, and in the process educate you in what your elders and betters thought were the ways of God. In some churches, the communication with God was the most important point; in others it was the education that was central.

The Muslims, with their praying openly five times a day no matter where they are, are an example to us. They are a reminder that God is not a one-day-in-seven God, but an everyday God. Yes, one day a week we should rest; that injunction seems based on a wisdom concerning the needs of the human body. But surely every day is holy, every day is God's day for those to whom God is real. How can we help to bring in God's domain (the "kingdom" of God, or what some are now calling the republic of God) unless we are in contact with God every day? We need that communication if we are to become the glorious people we have it in us to be, and if the world is to become the glory of related beings that it could be. Daily worship — giving worth to God — is no more a duty than eating meals every day is a duty: both the soul and the body need feeding. It need not consist of times of formal spoken prayer. What people sometimes call "communing with nature" can be part of that getting in touch with the larger reality that some of us call "God", and that can happen as we walk to work or look out of the window. Our contact with other people can be part of worship if we choose for it to be so, and we can do that by being aware of the God that is present in them also. A meal or a cup of coffee, whether we are alone or with others, can be sacramental by intention. Counting your blessings sounds horribly self-righteous, and yet it is very enriching. Even those in severe depression can be asked to think of one good thing in their present lives to thank God for, even if it is nothing more than the good cup of tea in their hands. Healthier people can stretch themselves to two or three things for which to give thanks.

Buildings for Worship

The buildings in which we meet to worship God are understandably precious to those who have known them for the greater part of their lives. The atmosphere, the very walls and furnishings that their eyes have rested on during years of faith and devotion, all serve to re-ignite fervent feelings. The sad thing is that, because of this, the buildings are often turned into idols. Their preservation becomes more important than the God for whose sake this action is ostensibly called. For every situation (and there are indeed some) where the determination to hold onto a particular building when it is virtually dead has brought new life to a congregation or community, there are all too many others where real harm has been done by the refusal to look to the greater good.

Some churches and chapels have an aura of prayer and godliness that is instantly recognised by the sensitive, and there is a good argument for keeping them as places of quiet even when the tide of community has gone from them. Many others seem to be soulless and often grim places, suggesting dour forms of religion and an unsmiling God. It is hard to see a future for them in any form of Christianity that might be expected to survive this century. If we are right to think that only a more right-brained, experiential Christianity will survive, it will not be helped by such buildings. Possibly they can be changed, if there is a common will for it, by re-ordering the spaces to provide communal seating and open areas, and light and colour, maybe even fire and water, and sight of earth and sky. Stained-glass windows have their admirers, but all too often in Irish churches and chapels, coloured glass has been used simply to block out the "distractions" of the beauty of God's world outside. I know a small oratory — a prayer room — in a monastic house in County Cork where the floor is carpeted and there are floor cushions and prayer stools as well as chairs, and the floor-to-ceiling window that is behind the Bible and the tabernacle looks out onto winding green fields and ancient trees, and the singing of the birds becomes part of the communal prayer.

It is not unthinkable that in the future worship will be approached very differently. If God were to become more of a natural part of our lives, it might be that we would not forever use special buildings to meet in, but would worship God in all places. But for as long as we do have chapels and churches, most will need at least some change if, instead of merely being museums of past religiosity, they are to entice and delight future Christians.

Relationship to God

Doctrine is not just the business of Church authorities. It affects us all and everything we do, including our attitude to God and the way we pray (or don't pray), because it affects our opinion of God and our opinion of ourselves. Certain doctrinal issues, such as the beliefs in life after death or in the presence of Christ in the bread and wine at the Eucharist, without a doubt affect our praying. Sometimes they will affect it for good, other times for ill. A belief in divine judgement on the Last Day will tend to produce in our lives a placatory attitude to God, an inclination to bury our talents for safe-keeping rather than to risk using them. On the other hand, for people to be able to believe that there is no anger in God, despite some words to that effect in the Bible, can be a huge release, out of fear and into creative love.

What we think about God determines the way we pray. Whether it is charismatic or contemplative prayer, adoration or homely chatting, or simply the type of prayer that is a list of requests, it will be influenced by our view of God. What image of God do we have in our heads in times of prayer? If it is an old man with a long beard that the eyes of our mind see, or a handsome young man in first-century robes, or a blank screen of dazzling light, then our praying will be fashioned accordingly. It is a principle of Judaism and Islam that no images of God should be made, since God is beyond our imaging. But Christianity has said that since Jesus brought God and the world together, "it is now possible to make an image of God".[12] I believe this has done serious damage, in that for many Christians the sole image they have of God is the human Jesus. "Your God is Too Small", J.B. Phillips famously said in his book of that title,[13] and certainly a 33-year old man in sandals, however holy, however God-filled, is too small an image to carry the vast unknowableness that we call God.

If the idea of the reality of God in any way draws people these days, it is the God of love that attracts, not the God of punishment. It is often said that people these days have no sense of guilt. Is this really so, or is it that they have a healthy level of awareness that they sometimes do wrong, and are sorry for it, without compounding that sorrow with the twisting fear of eternal punishment? Is it not just that a reaction to the over-production of guilt in the past has set in? Certainly, the present generation has more or less rejected the view of its forebears that we are all "miserable sinners". That rejection has been largely by way of anger. "I *not* naughty," the small child says to its parent. "I'm *not* bad," the people of the late twentieth century learned to say to God; and all too often they then walked away. The doctrine of Original Sin, developed to explain why there is indeed an impulse in even the best of people sometimes to go against goodness, was taken too far by the ecclesiastical control freaks of past centuries. Fortunately, in these days, even some bishops have taken against it:

> My problem with Christianity: You have to buy original sin as a reality, not as a fertile symbol or metaphor — and only when you do that, can you buy the whole edifice. That really is bad faith, an authoritarianism that no contemporary person can respect. Good faith, in my view, is about throwing things away all the time, not holding on to unjustifiable premises.[14]

But in the centuries when original sin was a serious matter, vices were written larger and larger, virtues made more impossible, and God turned into a more and more stern judge. For hundreds of years, there was intense theological argument going to and fro, backwards and forwards, as to how salvation was achieved: was it through faith, or was it through good works? Could you have faith in God and still be saved even if you didn't do any good works? Could you be saved by good works without faith? The terror of not achieving such "salvation" can be imagined when we look at some of the ancient paintings of sinners going down into hell, being tormented or torn apart by gleeful devils. Such paintings on church walls were the regular fare of illiterate Christians in the Middle Ages, and they appear to have been much more common than paintings of the blessed being received into heaven. So faith was ruled by fear, as it was even well into the twentieth century, driving many to be agonisingly scrupulous about their sins. Human nature finally rebelled in number-less Christians and overthrew such thinking. They were like Wonderland's Alice, saying to the creatures she was frightened of, "Why, you're nothing but a pack of cards!", and finding that no disaster resulted. But because it had needed the strength of rebellion, it very often also included the abandonment of all religious practice.

Two weapons in the fight against sin were preaching and confession. The second has always been the more important in the Catholic Church, and the first in the Protestant denominations. Catholics will often tell you that Protestants do not have confession and absolution, and many Protestants are under the same illusion. In fact, absolution following confession is available to Anglicans, which in Ireland means members of the Church of Ireland, and the ministry of absolution is listed among the "sacramental ministries of grace" in the Church of Ireland catechism. There is an Anglican saying as to who can avail themselves of it: "All can; none must; some should." Being optional has a good side and a not-so-good side. What is not so good is that, overall, very few members of Anglican churches make use of it. What is good is that because no-one is required to ask for it, there are no issues of clerical power attached to it.

The importance of the sermon in Protestantism, especially in the Presbyterian tradition, can never be underrated, and has at times included much hell-fire preaching. But just as Catholics think Protestants do not have confession, so Protestants are frequently under the impression that preaching is no real part of Catholicism. It may have been through a thin time in the past century, but as Vincent Ryan makes clear in his book *The Shaping of Sunday*, the Irish Church has a long history of respect for the exposition of Holy Scripture, placing it on a par with the Eucharist itself.[15]

Being able to feel good about ourselves is important if we are to build a better world. And feeling good about ourselves involves being able to recognise when we have been less than good, and make amends. Not by saying a few prayers to appease God, but actually putting right, to the best of our ability, whatever we have caused to go wrong. It is a shame that bad or inadequate administration of confession and absolution have led to its rejection by so many. There is enormous value in the practice: it allows someone to talk to another person, who is good and wise and non-manipulative; it allows them to discuss how they are getting on in their faith journey, so that the weak spots can be identified and acknowledged and new resolutions made and a blessing given and received. It seems to be on the increase in some places, as people become aware of the need, and search for the right person to become their "spiritual director" or "soul friend". The influence of psychology and also of the self-help books that fill the bookshops mean that people are aware of their own interior selves in a broader way than the old simplistic categorisations of goodness and badness. Correspondingly, the person chosen is no longer always an ordained person, and certainly not always male. It is good that people, whether lay or clergy, choose their own director or soul friend: most will know instinctively who is the right person for them. Often, it will be someone from a parish other than their own. There have been situations where Anglican clergy have been assigned a spiritual director at the time of their ordination. But such arranged relationships rarely last.

There was a time when the pursuit of holiness was a desirable quality in the religious life, and much attention was centred on it in spiritual direction. To modern minds, however, it seems somewhat self-centred, and a director or soul friend would be more likely to focus on right relationships with other people and the world around them. In the past, the lives of the saints were read as devotional encouragement and a spur to heroic holiness. Now that we know more about the psychology of human beings, more about the twistings and turnings of the human heart, we are less likely to assume that anyone is without the quirks and faults that make all of us less than angelic. We are more likely to be encouraged by those we know have done great things in spite of their all-too-humanness. Nevertheless, the present Pope has made more saints than any of his predecessors. The Protestant churches have never declared anyone a saint: the nearest the Anglican church has come to it has been the putting forward of various names for celebration in the Anglican Calendar. This has included people such as Hildegard, the twelfth-century visionary Abbess of Bingen; Elizabeth Fry, nineteenth-century prison reformer; and several from the twentieth century including Janani Luwum, the martyred Archbishop of Uganda; Simone Weil, the spiritual writer; theologian Dietrich Bonhoeffer; and Oscar Romero, the martyred Archbishop of San Salvador. It is worth noting that these and the many others on the calendar are by no means all Anglicans. In each of their lives they have shown something of the glory of God in many different ways and different situations. And they have all been people of prayer.

In a life set free from the sort of doctrine that ties us down and limits our perception of the glory of God, prayer becomes not less but more important. But for many, it is often a simpler prayer than the left-brain volumes of words that we have been taught in the past. It may be the way of prayer advocated by Jean Pierre de Caussade, of being aware of the divine in all things at all times, of what he called "the sacrament of the present moment".[16] It may be the way of prayer advocated by the seventeenth-century Brother Lawrence, who said that he was as much at home with God when he was working in the kitchens of the monastery as when he was on his knees in the chapel.[17] Or the way of the old man mentioned by the Curé d'Ars, who, when asked what he did while sitting at the back of the church all day and every day, said simply, "I look at Him, and He looks at me."

Most forms of Christian meditation are actually contemplative prayer, a state of wordless and imageless attention to God, beyond all doctrine and dogma. The development of networks of people of all denominations who pray in this way has been one of the religious phenomena of the twentieth century. Most of them have started out of a sort of starvation, out of the sense that the churches were not offering this type of prayer, had somehow written it off as suitable only for monks and nuns. Therefore those who had discovered it for themselves felt isolated. In some cases, they had even been told by their clergy that such prayer was "the work of the Devil", that by emptying their minds they would be letting the Devil in. Many have said that it was a source of relief and joy to them to find they were not alone in wanting to pray this way, and that they could occasionally share this praying with others as a support to their own daily practice of it. This quite widespread desire for utter silence is legitimate in its own right, having a long history within Christianity (as well as being common to most of the other world faiths). But it can also be seen as an obvious reaction to the over-wordy, over-doctrinised, left-brain liturgies that have for so long constituted worship in most of our churches.

Notes

---

[1] Matt 2:15, see also Hosea 11:1; Exodus 4:22.

[2] Alistair McIntosh, "Soil and Soul", (Aurum, 2001).

[3] Norvene Vest, *No Moment Too Small* (Cistercian Publications/Cowley Publications, 1994).

[4] Michel de Verteuil CSSp, *Your Word is a Light for My Steps: Lectio Divina* (Veritas, 1996).

[5] I am indebted to Fr John O'Connell DD for this information.

[6] *Catechism of the Catholic Church* (Geoffrey Chapman, 1995).

[7] Barnabas Lindars, in *A New Dictionary of Christian Theology*, edited by A. Richardson and J. Bowden (SCM Press, 1983).

[8] Garry Wills, *Papal Sin: Structures of Deceit* (Doubleday, 2000).

[9] Anglican-Roman Catholic International Commission, *The Final Report* (CTS/SPCK, 1982).

[10] National survey by the Center for Applied Research in the Apostolate, Washington DC, 2001.

[11] Arthur Peacocke, *Paths from Science Towards God* (Oneworld, 2001).

[12] Gregory Collins, OSB *The Glenstal Book of Icons* (Columba, 2002).

[13] J.B. Phillips, *Your God is Too Small* (Epworth Press, 1952).

[14] Bishop Richard Holloway, interviewed by Pat Kane in *The Independent*, 18 August 2001.

[15] Vincent Ryan OSB, *The Shaping of Sunday: Sunday and Eucharist in the Irish Tradition* (Veritas, 1997).

[16] Jean Pierre de Caussade, *Self-Abandonment to Divine Providence* (Tan Books, Illinois, 1959).

[17] Br Lawrence, *The Practice of the Presence of God*, trans. E.M. Blaiklock (Hodder & Stoughton, 1981).

Chapter 6

LIVING WITH EACH OTHER

"It is impossible to love Christ without loving others . . .
and it is impossible to love others . . . without moving
nearer to Christ." — *Pierre Teilhard de Chardin*[1]

When there are discussions about the benefits of Christian education, one of the arguments that people sometimes put forward in favour of it is that they want their children "to know the difference between right and wrong". The first time I heard that, when I was a curate, I was appalled that this was all that faith and religion seemed to mean to those who said it. With time, I came to respect that view, though I would still see it as very limited. The mistake is to suppose that good behaviour will happen as a result of being taught certain facts about God and religion and the Church. Good behaviour is, in the final analysis, the result of good relationships, with other human beings or with God or both.

What such comments are getting at, I think, is that the inevitable outcome of a keying-in to the divine presence in life is grace. And from grace proceeds goodness. If the relationship with the divine is very new or superficial, the goodness will be fragile. If the chosen image of the divine is skewed, the goodness will be skewed. But the more the relationship with a good image of the divine is developed, the stronger the tendency to goodness will be. In the story of Moses bringing the Ten Commandments down from the mountain where he has been speaking with God, it cannot be because they are apparently engraved in stone that the people want to obey those laws, but because they are the result of one man's contact with the Being who is above all knowledge, unseeable and awe-inspiring. In our own lifetimes, instructions to be good will have had no effect unless those who told us so were loved — or feared. Goodness through fear is a sad thing, and liable to rebound into badness. Goodness through love, whether human or divine, is both beneficial to all and lasting.

Christian education is full of commandments to be good. The biblical list we know as the Ten Commandments is usually taken from the Book of Deuteronomy 5:6–21, but is actually only one of several versions given in the Bible. A slightly different set appears in the Book of Exodus 20:1–17 and a very different set, which Christianity in the main ignores, occurs in Exod 34:11–26. This includes injunctions to keep the festival of unleavened bread for seven days, and not to boil a kid in its mother's milk. The following book, Leviticus, contains another set of about sixteen commandments given by God to Moses, which as well as requiring the people to honour their fathers and mothers, and not to steal, also tells them not to reap or gather all of their harvest but to leave some for the poor, not to eat anything with its blood, not to "round off the hair on your temples or mar the edges of your beard", and not to put on a garment made of two different materials.[2] In fact, the Book of Leviticus is full of rules, laws and instructions given by God to Moses, or to Moses and his brother Aaron, which Christianity sees no need to follow. For example:

> If the [leprous] disease breaks out again in the house, after he has taken out the stones and scraped the house and plastered it, the priest shall go and make inspection; if the disease has spread in the house, it is a spreading leprous disease; it is unclean. He shall have the house torn down, its stones and timber and all the plaster of the house, and taken outside the city to an unclean place.[3]

If, as Christians, we have no compulsion to obey some of those laws, it is surely because we have neither been taught them nor has our own personal experience of God suggested them. The Ten Commandments divide into a few laws concerning God — "make no images, keep the seventh day holy" — and the rest concerning human society. The latter make up a very workable programme for large groups of people to live together in harmony, which accounts for the fact that where the more esoteric commandments have failed to be taken up by Christianity, the Ten as we know them have survived the extension from Judaism into Christianity. They have a firm place in the Catholic and Orthodox and Anglican and Reformed churches, although with different degrees of emphasis.

Many of the principles of Christian ethics are found in the Sermon on the Mount, recorded in the Gospels of Matthew and Luke as having been given by Jesus. This includes eight or nine Beatitudes,[4] and many more teachings, the vast majority of which deal with social interaction. There are a few passages about relationship with God, and prayer. The "Our Father", or Lord's Prayer, is also part of the Sermon on the Mount,[5] although a longer version is found in Luke's gospel where it is given as Jesus' response to his disciples' request to teach them how to pray.[6]

In a larger sense, Christian ethics are drawn from the totality of the Gospels, not just from what Jesus said but from what he did. We learn how we should treat each other from the way in which Jesus is reported to have treated others, with the respect and care and love due to any other human being because he/she is a "child of the same heavenly Father". For Jesus, this did not depend on their place in society, or on their gender, or on their apparent sinfulness of goodness. For him, as for his Jewish ancestors, God's law could be explained in one phrase: to love God, and to love your neighbour.

In Roman Catholic theology, there are also the Commandments of the Church, sometimes known as the Precepts of the

Church, dating back to the Middle Ages. The four that are binding on all Catholics are: to attend Mass on all Sundays and Feasts of Obligation; to observe the days of fasting and abstinence; to go to confession at least once a year; and to receive holy communion during the Easter season. Additional precepts are added in various countries. These are ecclesiastical-spiritual rules rather than laws for healthy community relations, although their observance could be expected to have a good effect on society at large.

Relationships

Many of the disputes in our Churches for the past hundred years or so have related to personal relationships, particularly in the area of sexuality. In past centuries, such disputes centred on marriage, with the Church trying to maintain its authority in saying that a man and woman should not live together without having the relationship formalised by the Church. Among the poorer people, where property was not involved, there was quite commonly a reluctance to go along with this. But that was nothing compared to the upheavals that began early in the twentieth century. Simple and effective contraception became possible, with what we now see as huge consequences for the lives of women. After that, a multitude of related issues flooded in: sex before marriage, "living in sin", divorce, single motherhood, abortions and, eventually, same-sex relationships. On all of these matters, the Churches have had their say, with the pronouncements of the Catholic Church usually more severe than any put out by the Anglican or Reformed Churches. What gradually became apparent was that, whatever the doctrinal statements, most practising Christians said their prayers and then went along with their own consciences. Sex before marriage, living together without being married, divorce, and single motherhood are all quite normal in Ireland now. Abortion is still a contentious issue, with the moderate view being that it is always regrettable, and often emotionally damaging to the woman, but that very occasionally it is necessary. Divorce is another emotionally damaging process which may, however, in cases of cruelty or consistent unfaithfulness, be the lesser of two evils. But formal marriage is in any case on the decline throughout the Western world, as younger people in particular view it merely as a legal institution and see less and less need for it except as an excuse for a party. However, in Ireland there does still seem to be an awareness of a spiritual element to it in most cases.

Homosexuality and same-sex relationships are still in difficulty, both in the churches and in society as a whole. But little by little, public opinion is changing, legal opinion is following, and the churches will eventually catch up. There are many Catholics and Protestants who have been working for years for their churches to head up this change of attitude, not least because of their awareness of the number of gay men drawn to priesthood and ministry or to the religious orders. That they should have been forced to choose between either following their call but living lives of secrecy, or denying their vocation, is dreadful. There are of course religious organisations to which lesbians and gays can turn for mutual (and ecumenical) support,[7] but it is sad that they are needed. No-one chooses to be born gay, as even the Roman Catholic Catechism admits: yet many say that they have been aware of their condition since they were five or six years old. Scientists are discovering homosexuality in an increasing number of species of animals, suggesting it is an entirely natural condition. In other words, God has created a proportion of humans and animals predominantly or totally homosexual, and therefore with a need for same-sex relationships. Yet because they are a minority, they have been pilloried and discriminated against, just as left-handed people once were. "Ah, but it says in the Bible . . ." some say. Because people had such prejudices in biblical times is no excuse for our maintaining them now.

The recent election of an openly gay man as Bishop of New Hampshire, in the Episcopal Church of the United States of America, is set to cause huge problems for the Anglican Communion, because it focuses on the very question of whether all members of one Church can ever hold identical theological views. But many of us cannot help seeing this change as a hopeful step towards a more inclusive Church.

A good parent encourages goodness in a child by giving a high place to praise of whatever goodness they show, and a low place to disapproval of bad behaviour. What Christianity has tended to do is to give too much attention to what it thinks is wrong, and too little to praising the good. Of course, we need to recognise that we are not always good, and to acknowledge our thoughts and words and deeds that have fallen short of the mark, and done damage. Yet for far too many people, particularly women, the predominant sin is not having a good enough view of themselves. An example of this is that a common psychological reaction to abuse or rape is for the survivor to feel that they are in some way to blame. Tragically, the doctrine of Original Sin plays on this. A survivor of clerical sexual abuse said recently in a radio interview with Fergal Keane that it played a part in his own inability to escape from the abuse.

No wonder, then, that a book called *Original Blessing* had such an impact on the Catholic world at least — but also on various other Christians — when it was published in 1983. Written by Matthew Fox, who was at that time an American Dominican, it said that Catholic and Protestant teachings had for four centuries been concentrating on redemption theology and sanctification theology but ignoring creation theology. "Fall and redemption spirituality", Fox said, is suspicious, repressive, self-despising and elitist, with its emphasis on sin; whereas "creation-centred spirituality" is inclusive, accepting, celebratory, and with its emphasis on blessing.[8] The book is over-simplistic, especially in the way Fox divides people, past and present, into good guys and bad guys;

and many felt that the shallowness of his theology was too obviously a product of what the socialist theologian Kenneth Leech called "the unreal world of the eco-bourgeoisie".[9] All the same, the book in its heyday caused a healthy about-turn in the thinking of many Christians, and has had a continuing influence.

Whatever congregations say as they chant the creeds in church, few Christians now seriously believe that they are in any danger of going to hell when they die. Hell has largely been written out, except perhaps when it is recommended by tabloid newspapers for people whose evil actions they are headlining. (A survey of Irish people in 2003 found that only 37 per cent believe in hell.)[10] On the other hand, many seem to think that there is some sort of heaven for them to go to, where they will be reunited with their loved ones, even if they would not be able to describe that heaven. This gradual and independent change of thinking raises some interesting questions. Has it come about because people now believe in a totally loving God who could never sentence his creatures to eternal torment? Or is it because hell is now seen to have been an invented threat, part of the ecclesiastical control structures? And if it is no longer a threat, what effect has its loss had on individual behaviour, when Christian society is not noticeably more wicked than in previous generations? Or in other words, is a tendency to goodness and harmony with others simply built into us, rather than a response to the carrot-and-stick of a heaven and hell run by God?

The Domain (Kingdom, or Republic) of God

When millions of people in countries all over the world gather to protest against wars that they see as unnecessary or evil, and more millions respond to requests to provide food and water for fellow human beings facing drought or starvation, some would admit to doing so for "religious" reasons. Others would deny such motivation. Either way, what is going forward in such happenings is what has traditionally been called "the Kingdom of God". We need a better word now, when kingship denotes autocratic power out of keeping with our twenty-first century ideas of God. Yet this concept, which is central to the teachings of Jesus, is worth finding a new name for: it is as valid now as it was in his time. Some are using the word "Republic"; "Domain" is a possibility; there will be others. Whichever word we use, the concept is of the way of God taking precedence. At times, particularly in ancient Hebrew thought, it was a future event of reward for the righteous, which would follow the ending of the world and the Day of Judgement. In Christian terms, this was related to the anticipated "second coming" of Christ. At other times, the Kingdom of God has, astoundingly, been identified with the hierarchy of the Christian church. But Jesus spoke of it not only as a future event ("Thy Kingdom come" — Matthew 6:10) but also as something already in existence, although hidden ("the Kingdom of God is within you" — Luke 17:21). Indeed, that may have been his main emphasis. It has been suggested that

> . . . this conception of the Kingdom as a present reality occupied relatively a considerably more prominent place in the Lord's teaching than it fills in the Gospels and elsewhere in the [New Testament] where its centrality may have been displaced by the widespread expectation of the early Christians that a visible kingdom was on the point of appearing.[11]

For the new Christians, discovering its existence among us has a far greater resonance than any idea of living life in the expectation of its being revealed at the end of time.

Those of us who are middle-aged or older, whether Catholic or Anglican or Protestant, will have been brought up with the idea that somehow our worship of God was for God's benefit. But this encourages our picturing God as something quite separate from us. If, as Evelyn Underhill says, the object of worshipping God is the increase of love and the good of the world, then worship itself is a definite ingredient in the spread of God's domain. This is good. But what we are increasingly recognising is that protesting against war is also an ingredient, and so is helping to provide the necessities of life for those without them, and so is helping old ladies across the street, all regardless of the religion of those involved. The domain of God grows, and we recognise it in each other; and this recognition is becoming stronger in our societies, helping to dissolve the old barriers of the different faiths and religions.

Other barriers that are fading away are those between the established churches and the older and more traditional forms of respect for creation. No doubt the rejection of the left-brain culture of most organised religion has been a factor in the revival of paganism and wicca (modern witchcraft) with their emphases on the connection between ourselves, our bodies, and the natural world. Science and ecology support this, constantly reminding us that we are part of nature. The various threats posed to the earth's fragile ecosystem have played a part in this move to an "earth-centred" religion. And in fact much of what we do in the Church is not a million years distanced from paganism. One example is the way our church buildings look to the east. We tell ourselves, or we are told, that we are facing Jerusalem: but all over the world religious people face the rising sun, showing how instinctively our bodies are connected to the workings of the planet.

Some Christians are frightened of words like "pagan" or "wicca", but many others are seeing by reflection our own past failures in relation to the natural world. We have paid lip service to the sacredness of creation, while ignoring the damage that is done to it by commerce and greed. Our theology has been concerned with our own personal salvation and little, if at all, with the salvation of that which we say God created. We have been shamed by young men and women in scruffy clothes risking their lives to save trees or protect wildlife. We have done the very opposite, deriding the beauties of creation, considering them dangerous to our salvation. The ecclesiastical authorities have shut them out of our church buildings, by having windows high up in the walls and even filling them with coloured glass; anything to keep out the sight of the sky and the trees. In many of our dark and gloomy churches, parishioners say on a nice day, "Couldn't we be outside?" and they are only half joking. Now increasing numbers are turning their backs on these haughty buildings, and are meeting for worship and real community in outdoor places or in each others' houses. In gatherings like these, there are no doctrinal or denominational tests for membership. No authority is required. Anyone who wants to join in is welcomed, and everyone's gifts are respected. Bishops and clerics and reactionaries may fight it, but this could indeed be the Christianity of the future, the Christianity which will survive.

Notes

[1] P. Teilhard de Chardin, *Le Milieu Divin* (Fontana, 1964).

[2] Lev. 19:2–37.

[3] Lev. 14:43–45.

[4] Matthew 5:3–12.

[5] Matthew 6:9–13.

[6] Luke 11:2–4.

[7] For example: Reach, c/o Outhouse, 105 Capel Street, Dublin 1; and, the Lesbian & Gay Christian Movement, Oxford House, Derbyshire Street, London E2 6HG.

[8] Matthew Fox, *Original Blessing* (Bear & Co., Santa Fe, New Mexico, 1983).

[9] Angela West, *Matthew Fox: Blessing for Whom?*; introduction by Kenneth Leech (Blackfriars Publications, n.d.).

[10] The Diageo Ireland Quality of Life Report 2003 (www.amarach.com).

[11] F.L. Cross, ed., *Oxford Dictionary of the Christian Church* (Oxford University Press, 1958).

Chapter 7

WHAT IS TRUTH?

"I still have many things to say to you, but you cannot bear
them now. When the Spirit of truth comes, he will guide
you into all the truth." — *John 16:12–13*

It might not be an overstatement to say that all the so-shameful
wars of religion that have happened down through the ages
and on into our own time have been the result of one or (more
usually) both sides claiming to have the true truth, the only truth.
There are of course always other factors, such as tribalism parad-
ing as faith, or material gain hiding under ideologies. But the
common thread is surely this conviction that the view of God that
we have been educated into is the right one, and therefore by
definition all the others must be wrong. And God would want us
to fight for the truth. *Our* truth.

Victor Griffin, who for 22 years was Dean of St Patrick's Cathedral, Dublin, and before that had worked for 22 years in Derry,
says:

> How we speak of God must always be partial, never final,
> the last word. For churches to claim finality or absolute cer-
> tainty for their partial understanding leads to exclusiveness
> and religious self-righteousness which can easily, when
> mixed with tribal politics, degenerate into sectarianism.[1]

By whatever workings of humanity, or social psychology, or that
mysterious thing, morphic resonance — or maybe even the work-

ing of the spirit of God? — we seem to be coming through to widespread mutual agreement that one person's truth does not automatically invalidate another person's truth. In England, the Chief Rabbi, Jonathan Sacks, was in serious trouble recently with some of his friends in Orthodoxy for suggesting that Judaism does not contain all the truth.

> In heaven there is truth; on earth there are truths. . . . God is greater than any religion . . . He is only partially comprehended by any faith. He is my God, but also your God. He is on my side, but also on your side.[2]

He was under pressure to withdraw what he had written, but no matter: that opinion is already out there, working away, having its healthy effect on us all. From the Professor of Judaism at the University of Wales had come a similar opinion:

> Neither Jew, nor Muslim, Christian, Hindu nor Buddhist has any justification for believing that his or her respective tradition embodies the uniquely true and superior religious path. Adherents of all faiths must recognise the inevitable human subjectivity of religious conceptualisation. This recognition calls for a complete reorientation of religious apprehension. What is now required is for Jews and Christians at least to acknowledge that their conceptual systems, forms of worship, lifestyles, and scriptures are nothing more than lenses through which divine reality is perceived, but that the divine as it is itself is beyond human understanding.[3]

Within Christianity, the battle for this view of truth is already won in some places. The ecumenical movement in its good days had fostered the thinking that we should not be aiming for a unanimous Christian theology or a homogenous way of being Church, but that we should be aiming for, and delighting in, "diversity in unity". In other places it is only just beginning, and the wrestling is all still to do. The necessity of what John Hick calls a uniform belief-system is still taken for granted by many, but is called into question by increasing numbers.

> The question of how the lordship of Jesus . . . is to be understood philosophically was the subject of a tremendous many-sided debate in the early Christian centuries, which was only "settled" when the Roman Emperor insisted upon a uniform belief-system for Christendom. But there have always been those who have been dissatisfied with the official formulae; and now that such dissenters are no longer burned at the stake, they are more numerous than ever.[4]

From a Benedictine background, Sr Joan Chittister says:

> People currently considered "excommunicated" or "suspect" or "heretical" or "smorgasbord" believers are, in many ways, among the most intense Christians of our time. They do more than sing in the choir or raise money for the parish centre or fix flowers for the church. They care about it and call it to be its truest self. They question it, not to undermine it, but to strengthen it. They call for new ways of being church together. They do not dismiss the need for the spiritual life. They crave it. What's more, they look for it in their churches. But they crave more than ritual. They crave meaning. They look for more than salvation. They look for authenticity and the integrity of the faith.[5]

The doctrine of papal infallibility is a relatively new one (Pius IX, 1870), suggesting a degree of anxiety about the acceptance or otherwise of doctrinal statements by the faithful. It is to the present Pope's credit that he is said to have claimed he would never use it. On the other hand, the widespread distress at his recent encyclical *Ecclesia de Eucharistia*, re-emphasising the teaching that Catholics may not receive holy communion in "ecclesial communities separated from the Catholic Church" (i.e. in non-Catholic Churches), because they "lack a valid sacrament of orders", is an indication that the faithful are more and more liable to trust their own understanding of what is right. What seems to be coming through, in all this, is a sense that those who are drawn to God and/or goodness have an intuitive understanding of what that says to them, an intrinsic or internal state of truth appreciation. Beliefs "declared" by the Bible or the Church, on the other hand, are extrinsic, coming from outside the individual and being imposed upon them. In past generations, under the power of clerical paternalism, this was accepted, and those beliefs were internalised. But now the extrinsic truth must coincide with the intrinsic truth if it is to be adopted. In other words, the days of "Believe this because we tell you to" are over.

And the "truths" that we accept are now more fluid than the concrete statements of past times. As we are exposed in our ever more interracial, inter-faith world to more and more different cultures, so we are increasingly aware of the tentativeness of the truths we hold. As far back as sixty years ago, the Protestant theologian Reinhold Niebuhr was writing:

> However we twist or turn, whatever instruments or pretensions we use, it is not possible to establish the claim that we have the truth. The truth remains subject to the paradox of grace. We may have it; and yet we do not have it. And we will have it the more purely in fact if we know that we have it only in principle. Our toleration of truths opposed to those which we confess is an expression of the spirit of forgiveness in the realm of culture. Like all forgiveness, it is possible only if we are not too sure of our own virtue.[6]

In our own time, the scientist Arthur Peacocke talks about "sufficient truth":

> Absolute truth is unattainable; but sufficient truth by which to live meaningfully and consistently with what we can best infer about the realities and the Ultimate Reality in which we live is worth seeking.[7]

And the former Archbishop of York is saying something similar when he says:

All truth depends upon metaphor, because only through metaphor is it possible to imagine the unimaginable.[8]

So, bit by bit, we are learning a new approach to the word "truth". We are beginning to see that the old approach has been oversimplified and too damagingly direct. That does not mean we should therefore simply shrug our shoulders and give up thinking about it all. Long ago the Anglican theologian Maurice Wiles said that there was work to be done, and warned that not everyone would approve:

> It is worthwhile [for the doctrinal critic who is also a Christian] to worry away at what lies at the heart of, underneath, or at the back of, traditional doctrinal statements; in their old form they may no longer make satisfactory sense for him in relation to his honest attempts to understand the world in which he lives in all its depth, but that is not the same thing as to say that he regards them as unimportant or valueless. . . . Every Christian theologian must expect the charge of being unfaithful either to the historical tradition of Christian faith or to the realities of the modern world. But that is no argument against the propriety of the task.[9]

It is perhaps unrealistic to expect change to come from the top. Again and again, the churches have been made aware of ancient doctrinal statements which are actually causing damage by not being withdrawn; but, as with the Thirty-Nine Articles, they have put their heads into the sand, preferring not to think about them. Dr Giles Fraser sees a significant difference here between truth and truthfulness. Truthfulness, he says, we find much more problematic than the notion of truth. He gives as an example the document *Issues in Human Sexuality* which was drawn up by the bishops of the worldwide Anglican Church, and which contains some now-famous double-thinking on the subject of homosexuality:

> . . . our bishops are obliged publicly to defend the patent nonsense that is *Issues in Human Sexuality*. It is news to no-

one that a great many bishops think this document nonsense, too. None the less, in the Church truthfulness is
sometimes seen as a private luxury, an indulgence, even,
that draws attention away from our witness to the Truth itself. Or, to put it barely: the church is better at truth than it
is at honesty (truthfulness).[10]

So we come back to the observation that people in all our
churches, tired of waiting for the ecclesiastical hierarchies to make
the obvious and necessary changes, are right on the verge of de-
ciding that they will find what is the truth for them.

Today, intelligently educated but often theologically unin-
formed people, if they are still attached in any way to the Christian churches, are hanging on by their fingertips as they
increasingly bracket off sections of the liturgies in which they par-
ticipate as either unintelligible, or unbelievable in their classic
form, or both (e.g., the virginal conception of Jesus; the resurrection of the body; the use of sacrificial, substitutionary and propi-
tiatory imagery with respect to Jesus' death; and much else).[11]
"Should anyone believe anything that isn't self-evident?", Sr Joan
Chittister asks.

What are waitresses and cab drivers and young teachers and
old grandparents and secretaries and accountants and parents of
small children supposed to believe when all the professional believers of the world disagree? And what is belief anyway? And
should anyone believe anything that isn't self-evident? Is it any
longer credible, in fact, to believe in faith, to have faith in belief? Is
creed even possible now?[12]

Looked at objectively, there is nothing to stop the faithful from
going their own, new way except a fear of abandoning the infan-
tile dependency they were brought up in — or nostalgia. Once the
myth of a perfect priesthood is exploded, as has now so painfully
happened, all the other "truths" in Catholicism are up for ques-
tioning, even if at first there is reluctance or resistance. The Anglican and Protestant equivalent is that the rectors and ministers

were formerly considered to be more educated than the lay people, and therefore their exposition of theological "truths" went unchallenged. Now, with religious matters regularly aired on television and radio and in the newspapers and magazines, not to mention easily available books, everyone can be their own theologian. The rectors and ministers are being challenged — or left high and dry.

It is clear that the map of truth is being redrawn in this third millennium. Partly it is that vast, and seemingly recent, changes in our understanding of the universe have affected what goes on in the universe of our own minds. But also it is that these changes have actually been affecting thinking people for more than two centuries, while the Church hierarchies have been refusing to face up to them. The Emperor has had to be seen to be wearing his marvellous suit. The hierarchies are now reaping the result of that refusal, with the drying-up of the old form of Christianity under their feet. Will it shrink to nothing, leaving them stranded? Or is it yet possible for them to open the doors of truth to all, and for everyone to be allowed to wander in and look around and find treasures?

What is truth, for us, now?

Can it be different for different people, and still be "true"?

We need to be able to allow diversity of thinking.

We need to be able to talk about all this.

Notes

[1] Victor Griffin, *Enough Religion to Make Us Hate* (Columba, 2002).

[2] Jonathan Sacks, *The Dignity of Difference* (Continuum, 2002).

[3] Dan Cohn-Sherbok, "A mystery beyond our conception", in *The Church Times*, 25 January 2002. —see p. 142

[4] John Hick, *The Second Christianity* (SCM, 1983).

[5] Joan Chittister OSB, *In Search of Belief* (Redemptorist Publications, 1999).

[6] Reinhold Niebuhr, *The Nature and Destiny of Man*, Vol. II (Nisbet & Co., London, 1943).

[7] Arthur Peacocke, *Paths from Science Towards God* (Oneworld, 2001).

[8] John Habgood, "Help with saying the unsayable", in *The Church Times*, 3 January 2003.

[9] Maurice Wiles, *Working Papers in Doctrine* (SCM, 1976).

[10] Giles Fraser, "Truthful — In My Fashion", in *The Church Times*, 21 March 2003.

[11] Arthur Peacocke, *Paths from Science Towards God* (Oneworld, 2001).

[12] Joan Chittister, OSB, *In Search of Belief* (Redemptorist Publications, 1999).

Chapter 8

CHRISTIANITY OF THE FUTURE

"The Church is the Church only when it exists for others."
— *Dietrich Bonhoeffer*

The days of regulated and uniform thinking within a church or organisation are over. We all have different perceptions, different understandings, of God and of "the things of God", and we can no longer *either* pretend to uniform thinking *or* hand over our brains to "those who really know". The Church as a whole is not facing up to this. But some clergy, like Graham Shaw, are:

> There is a tendency both in the pew and the pulpit to hope that if atheism is ignored it will somehow go away. Indeed that rather pathetic hope is often mistaken for faith. The stubborn reassertion of traditional theism is comforting and makes few demands of either the speaker or the listener. Questioning and reconstructing inevitably disturb and can easily be disparaged as negative and destructive. . . . I do not believe that widespread indifference means the end of religion, but I suspect that it points to a rather different religion, in which some aspects of our inherited belief in God will be discarded, and others will possess a new cogency.[1]

And scientists, like Arthur Peacocke, are also speaking out loud and clear:

> What we all have to do in this interaction of theology with the sciences is, by argument and imagination, to develop a concept of God, belief in the reality of whom is consistent

with what we now know from science about the cosmos, this planet and our own arrival here . . . We require an open, revisable, exploratory, radical — dare I say it? — liberal theology. This may well be unfashionable among Christians who seem everywhere to be retreating into the fortresses of Protestant evangelicalism, traditional (Anglo-) Catholicism and/or so-called "biblical theology". Nevertheless, transition to such a theology is, in my view, unavoidable if Christians in the West, and eventually elsewhere, are not to degenerate in the new millennium into an esoteric society internally communing with itself and thereby failing to transmit its "good news" (the *evangel*) to the universal (*catholicos*) world. . . . For such a Christian theology to have any viability, it may well have to be stripped down to newly conceived basic essentials.[2]

Plenty of journalists, like Andrew Brown, have sensible things to say, too:

What would be interesting and genuinely new would be a bishop who not only refrained from telling us things that no grown-up thinks are true, but who managed to say new things that grown-ups thought might be true and Christian as well. Perhaps it's impossible.[3]

The Christian Church is faced now with a huge choice: to change or to die. Jack Spong, former Episcopalian (Anglican) Bishop of Newark, New Jersey, has been saying this for many years, notably in his book *Why Christianity Must Change or Die*,[4] but also in newspaper and magazine articles:

I believe that Christianity stands on the verge of a great transformation, in which the power of Christ will be separated from the institution that calls itself the body of Christ. The Christianity that cannot change will surely die. The choice is to bring on the reformation or stand by in pious inertia. I cast my vote for reformation.[5]

What stands in the way of change seems on the surface to be to do with theology. But just below the surface lies the real impediment — power.

> Ancient religion in both its Jewish and its Gentile forms was concerned with power. . . . The divine was conceived as the source of the power that human beings possessed . . . The common religious structure, shared by Jew and pagan alike, promised privilege and power, so that its leaders exercised control over society . . . In many of its aspects Christianity is the heir of the same religious tradition. . . . [It] demanded total conformity to its public rituals and achieved . . . a control of behaviour and disposition as pervasive as that of the Jewish Law. . . . I have spoken of all these things as if they belonged to a past which had vanished; I wish that might be so, but it is not the case. In many of its manifestations today Christianity remains unrepentantly a religion of power.[6]

The American James Carroll, a former priest and still a committed Catholic, also sees power as the primary cause of what has gone wrong in the Church:

> Once the myth of the perfect parent [i.e. in the priesthood] is broken, the young can grow into adulthood, taking responsibility for themselves. Catholics can never regard priests and bishops uncritically again, nor can they cooperate any longer in the small dishonesties that have spawned such massive betrayal . . . A power structure that is accountable only to itself will always end by abusing the powerless. Even then, it will paternalistically ask to be trusted to repair the damage. Never again.[7]

These are fairly recent writings. Yet radical proposals for the Church of the future were being made 50 years earlier. Dietrich Bonhoeffer wrote from prison:

> The Church is the Church only when it exists for others. To make a start, it should give away all its property to those in need. The clergy must live solely on the free-will offerings of their congregations, or possibly engage in some secular calling. . . . Our Church, which has been fighting in these years only for its own self-preservation, as though that were an end in itself, is incapable of taking the word of reconciliation and redemption to mankind and the world. . . . Any attempt to help the Church prematurely to a new expansion of its organization will merely delay its conversion and purification.[8]

The seeds of the new Church are already being sown. Already more and more Christians are meeting together in small groups, often regardless of denomination, gathering for reading and prayer and worship and a meal or refreshments with social interaction. In these groups they give and receive support and care that cover both their spiritual and their secular concerns. No one is in charge. No-one is spiritually superior. All are perceived as having gifts to offer. These groups give every indication of being the Church of the future, attracting those who are distressed by the way their own churches are refusing to move or grow. Yet such people are loyal to their tradition and can bring its riches to share with others. Ecumenism from the top-down has come to very little: there are too many vested interests. What seems to be happening now is that impatient people at the grassroots are creating their own ecumenism.

If the Church is to change and live, what will go? If the change is brought about by the laity simply walking away from what they can no longer tolerate, then probably the following three things will go:

- The power structures, which have in so many places encouraged — or even necessitated — deceit, hypocrisy and dishonesty;

- The paternalism, wherever it still exists, which is a by-product of the power structures: it has kept far too many Christians in spiritual childishness;

- The imposition of doctrines formulated long ago and in another culture, which no longer ring true to vast numbers both inside and — consequentially — outside the Church.

With the middle ground of Christianity slowly dying out, it looks as if there are two forms of the Church that are likely to survive. One is the reactionary (going backwards and tightening up), the other is the progressive (going forwards and loosening up). The first tends to be clergy-led, the second is mostly led by the laity. The first can include fundamentalists, the second can include near-atheists. An example of the reactionary type can be seen in a small book called *The Future of Religion* by Fr Felipe Fernández-Armesto. The author starts by saying that people want sacraments and liturgy, not theology and doctrine. But his "Five reasons for faith in the future of faith" are more ominous. These are: that "the unintelligible cosmos disclosed by postmodern science and philosophy will drive people back to the comforting certainties of suprarational faith"; that "in a morally deprived world societies will need moral dogma to survive, and individuals will want peremptory[9] guidance to relieve their bewilderment"; that "apocalyptic forebodings aroused by the pace of change and the vulnerability of a small world will concentrate minds on eternity"; that "demographic trends in the developed world will favour traditional religion"; and that "religions that get distracted by worldly objectives will not be likely to do secular jobs well . . . righting the world is not what religions do best and people still want heaven".[10]

Such wistful longing to be back in the past with all the certainties of its authoritarianism and other-worldliness will certainly find echoes in a lot of hearts, and many, including those with vested interests, will want to encourage such thinking. No doubt small pockets of this form of religion will survive for a while. And — more damagingly — the extreme fundamentalist forms will survive perhaps longer. Neither of these examples could be said to be healthy forms. We cannot go backward into the future.

If moderate Christianity is to continue to exist, it is likely to be as a loose federation. It will consist of those who are impressed by the teachings of Jesus of Nazareth and would like to follow them, while holding a diversity of theological views: the Church can no longer set out specific doctrines and demand that Christians believe them. Nor can it any longer demand that Christians contain themselves obsequiously within its structures. Yet community will still be needed and desired. Alan Jamieson, in his excellent book on what happens to people who leave EPC (Evangelical, Pentecostal and Charismatic) churches, says, "The majority of church leavers I have met either are or want to be part of post-church groups . . . not connected to any institutional form of the church or church structures." Elsewhere, he gives the figure for that majority as 74 per cent. All the post-church groups he mentions had been formed to provide a forum to discuss topics and issues not normally up for discussion in EPC churches. This will often be in the format of breakfast-with-discussion, followed by a worship service of their own arranging. Such liminal or threshold groups, Jamieson says:

> . . . can provide glimpses of new ways of constructing and nurturing Christian faith. . . . Where the liminal groups have let go of the dead faith, practices and structures of the EPC churches that have to them become oppressive and destructive, we may find indications of ways of doing church that will connect with many in our wider society. If so, such liminal groups are prophetic in their existence . . .[11]

What does this say to the EPC churches themselves? Should it be business as usual? The leavers indicate that this is not possible, he says. There is a suspicion now of evangelism and conversion: what is favoured instead is faith development and maturity. "The degree of fundamental change required should not be underestimated."

For those leaving all types of churches, a new community perhaps becomes even more desirable when entrants are no longer required to say they believe what in honesty they know they do not believe, and when they know they will be able to air their thoughts openly. But such communities will be formed naturally, without instructions from outside, and will be autonomous. (Or at least they will be so at the beginning. There is of course always the danger that in time they will be taken over by power factions and become institutions like the churches they replaced.)

So what will remain of Christianity in the future? If we are talking about an organic process that is already underway, then none of us can predict the eventual shape of it. But here are some probabilities:

- A full acknowledgement of the divine presence that is part of all creation, and the special historical-traditional place of Jesus in our faith-culture;

- An acknowledgement of the tasks that the awareness of this presence lays on us;

- Communities of faith, supporting each other with minimal organisation and no openings for power-grabbing;

- And therefore, if communities are so large that they need a full-time worker, that person will probably be an administrator, not a clergy person;

- Gatherings for worship as and when that particular faith-community chooses, in whatever place they choose, and with whatever content they choose;

- Membership of the faith-community open to all, with no credal requirements, so that to want to be part of it is all that is needed;

- Contacts to enable all these autonomous communities to be in touch with each other, so that they do not do separately what they could better do together — but with no hierarchical structures.

To enlarge on these points:

Beliefs

Every person's image of God, ideas about God, and relationship with God is influenced by their own personality and experiences as well as by what they have learnt from others. In a mature community, this is accepted and respected. No longer, in the future church, will the ideas of one individual or one group be considered to be the one exclusive truth. In Jack Spong's words, freeing Christianity from the shackles of the past, so that it can live in a new form in the future, involves:

> . . . conceiving of God beyond the traditional definitions of the theistic deity, and seeing the Christ not as the incarnation of that theistic deity but as a doorway into the fullness of life . . . as a god presence erupting within humanity, inviting us into the experience of living fully, and having the courage to be all that each of us is capable of being.[12]

Action

When attention to the divine produces impulses to action, such as humanitarian aid, or political protest, or the establishment of facilities for those in need in the secular community, there is usually strength in numbers. The churches of the past have a good record of such response, and it can only increase when people are empowered by each one taking responsibility for the work of their faith-community.

Communities of Faith

One of the things that feminism has pointed up is that it is the masculine structure of organisation which has tended to predominate in western society. In this, power is at the top, and filters diminishingly downwards. But this is not the only way. Women, unless they are aping male structures, will tend to work together, sharing decision-making and with each one taking on specific tasks. Administration is minimalised. Increasingly, this second way is being adopted by all sorts of organisations, and will surely be the way of the faith-communities of the future.

Clergy

In such a community, the clergy (if that word survives at all) will not be the overall head but a man or woman with, like everyone else, a specific task. They will probably be chosen by the community, and trained in leading worship and in the encouragement of spirituality and action but will keep to their secular livelihood. They will not have any responsibility for the premises, if any, in which the community meets, or for any administrative work. They will not be solely responsible for the pastoral work of the community: this will be undertaken by those members of the community who have a talent for it. One of the long-time problems with having a professional paid ministry is that there is at present a tendency, once clergy are ordained, for their theology — which up until then has been a living growing thing — to turn to stone because they sense consciously or unconsciously that further growth might open paths out of the ministry and therefore out of a job. In a more equal community, this would be less likely: the priest or minister would be able to develop naturally, to the benefit of all; and to move on, if that became desirable, without loss of livelihood. A related problem is that, because they are always functioning as leaders of worship, clergy are liable to find their own spirituality less than adequately fed.

Worship

Older people in our churches sometimes complain that the words of church services are being tinkered with too much and too often. For scientist Arthur Peacocke, the tinkering is too small.

> Even well meaning, recent liturgical revision . . . savours too much of an exercise in rearranging the deckchairs as the *Titanic* goes down. A liturgy can be meaningful only when it relates to what can be defended as public truth — all else is in danger of becoming the mere whistling in the dark of a beleaguered minority.[13]

The nature of worship in the emerging Church varies from group to group. It usually consists of some or all of the following: readings, singing, silence, prayer formal and informal, art, representations of nature, music and movement, communal meals. In the church of the future, some will take place in people's homes, as with the existing groups, some in churches or chapels, some perhaps outdoors. Sometimes it will be shaped by the minister or priest, at other times by one or more members of the group. A wider variety of liturgical forms, old and new, would ensure that all Christians are provided for, all are fed.

Membership

One of the great benefits of membership of a faith-community is that even in the private practice of prayer and ethics and individual social action there is the knowledge that others are similarly engaged. An apparent downside of the membership being open to anyone is that difficulties will occasionally arise among the members. However, coping with these in the group, without relying on a leader, and coming through to improved relationships, actually strengthens the group.

The Wider Church

There are already in existence several religious bodies, such as Judaism, and Islam, and the Society of Friends (Quakers), which have no supreme head and, in varying degrees, no one overall administration. The emerging Christian church will probably follow the same pattern. The obvious model is that of Celtic Christianity, where the churches were part of a network which centred on the local monastery. Without romanticising the concept, it is possible to see that in such a system it is spirituality that is at the centre, symbolised by people in simple clothing saying their prayers and doing ordinary work. This is in contrast to the Roman model that eventually overthrew the Celtic, setting up a system centred on the worldliness of the great cathedrals, with mitres and thrones for its bishops and grand houses for its clergy. Communication between the Christian faith-communities is obviously valuable, as is the organisation of conferences and special-interest meetings across geographical areas and interfaith boundaries. Social action will often be better done by several communities working together. Contact between the communities is necessary for all these reasons.

None of this is going to be easy. It would be foolish to ignore the fact that the transition will be in many ways a painful process, even to being a "dark night of the soul" for the Church. Yet when St John of the Cross used that much misused expression, he was talking about the necessary painfulness of the transition to new life.

Contrary to popular thinking, ideas of God and of the Church have never been fixed but have changed continuously through the ages. We are on the edge now of another large shift, and we need courage to go with it so that at last honest new faith can be planted, and new growth follow. Ultimately, we must decide to hold to the core of our belief, which sustains and enables us, and that is quite simply our belief in God. We need to hold on without demanding to be in control of God by understanding and defining God. "If you understand, it is not God," as St Augustine so amazingly said. Maybe a prayer from the fourteenth century helps us to simplify our approach to the divine:

> God, of your goodness give me yourself.
> For I may ask nothing that gives less than full worthship to you.
> If I ask for anything less, I will be always in want.
> Only in you do I have all.
>
> — *Julian of Norwich*

Notes

[1] Graham Shaw, *God in Our Hands* (SCM, 1987).

[2] Arthur Peacocke, *Paths from Science Towards God* (Oneworld, 2001).

[3] Andrew Brown, "The Press" columnist, in *The Church Times*, 7 September 2001.

[4] John Shelby Spong, *Why Christianity Must Change or Die* (Harper, 1988).

[5] "The church is dead, long live the reformation", in *The Guardian*, 9 December 2000.

[6] Graham Shaw, *God in Our Hands* (SCM, 1987).

[7] James Carroll, *Toward a New Catholic Church* (Houghton Mifflin, 2002).

[8] Dietrich Bonhoeffer, *Letters and Papers from Prison* (SCM Press, 1953).

[9] Peremptory: "admitting of no contradiction".

[10] Felipe Fernández-Armesto, *The Future of Religion* (Orion Publishing, 1997).

[11] Alan Jamieson, *A Churchless Faith: Faith Journeys beyond the Churches* (SPCK, 2002).

[12] "The church is dead, long live the reformation", in *The Guardian*, 9 December 2000.

[13] Arthur Peacocke, *Paths from Science Towards God* (Oneworld, 2001).

SUGGESTED FURTHER READING

Carroll, James, *Towards a New Catholic Church* (Houghton Mifflin, 2002).

Chittister, Joan, *In Search of Belief* (Redemptorist Press, 1999).

Hay, David, *Religious Experience Today* (Mowbray, 1990).

Jamieson, Alan, *A Churchless Faith: Faith Journeys Beyond the Churches* (SPCK, 2002).

O'Leary, Daniel, *Passion for the Possible* (Columba, 1998).

Richards, Clare, *Introducing Catholic Theology* (Kevin Mayhew, 2002).

Robinson, John A.T., *Honest to God* (SCM Press, 1963).

Smith, Adrian B., *A New Framework for Christian Belief* (CANA, 2001); available from CANA, 102 Church Road, Steep, Petersfield, Hants GU32 2DD, UK.

Spong, John Shelby, *Why Christianity Must Change or Die* (Harper Collins, NY, 1998).

Advanced Reading

Hick, John (ed.), *The Myth of God Incarnate* (SCM Press, 1977).

Macquarrie, John, *Jesus Christ in Modern Thought* (SCM Press, 1990).

Montefiore, Hugh, *Looking Afresh: Soundings in Creative Dissent* (SPCK, 2003).

Peacocke, Arthur, *Paths from Science Towards God* (Oneworld, 2001).

Tillich, Paul, *The Shaking of the Foundations* (SCM Press, 1949; Penguin, 1963).

Turner, Denys, *The Darkness of God: Negativity in Christian Mysticism* (Cambridge University Press, 1995).

If any readers would like to share their thoughts about this book with the author, she can be contacted by e-mail at wakeman@iolfree.ie

INDEX

Aaron, 132
abortion, 134
Abraham, 66, 100
Acts of the Apostles, 63, 90, 91, 95, 104
Adam and Eve, 55, 69, 85, 86, 87, 108, 111
Andersen, Hans Christian, 3, 13
angels, 28, 45, 69, 80, 100, 109
Anglicanism, 5, 11–12, 19, 25, 26–9, 30, 31, 32, 38, 57, 83, 113, 116, 117, 118, 125, 126, 127, 128, 133, 134, 136, 138, 145, 146, 150
anointing of the sick, 113
Anselm, St, 20, 85
Apollinarianism, 23
apophaticism, 52
Aquinas, St Thomas, 1, 20, 30, 52, 83
ARCIC (Anglican and Roman Catholic International Commission), 116
Arianism, 22
art and artistic expression, 8, 20, 21, 42, 60, 97, 109, 118, 158
Artaud, Antonin, 109
ascension, 26, 95
atheism, 149, 153

atonement, substitutionary, 31, 48, 84, 85, 87, 88
Augustine, St, 1, 52, 160
Augustus, Emperor, 79
authority and authoritarianism, 4, 6, 10, 17, 18, 37, 41, 50, 74, 92, 114, 124, 134, 140, 149, 153

Balasuriya, Tissa, 29
baptism, 16, 22, 42, 43, 113, 119
Beatitudes, 133
belief, *vii*, *viii*, 3, 4, 5, 6, 7, 8, 10, 15–32, 40, 45, 46, 47, 48, 54, 58, 60, 63, 65, 66, 74, 75, 76, 77, 88, 89, 92, 93, 96, 99, 100, 101, 102, 107, 112, 116, 117, 123, 137, 143, 144, 146, 149, 150, 154, 155, 159
  changing nature of, 31
  expressing, 7, 8, 11, 17, 19, 22, 37, 47, 48, 49, 75, 77, 80, 116
Bible, 9, 11, 17, 18, 19, 24, 25, 28, 30, 40, 47, 48, 49, 51, 54, 57, 67, 98, 99, 100, 101, 102, 104, 107, 108, 109, 110, 111, 112, 122, 123, 132, 135, 144
  as divinely inspired, 107
  inerrancy of, 19, 30
  reading the, 107–11
biblical scholarship, 18, 68

Also available from The Liffey Press

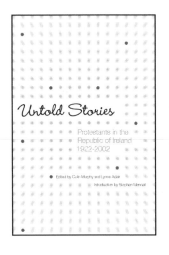

Untold Stories

Protestants in the Republic
of Ireland 1922–2002

Edited by Colin Murphy
and Lynne Adair

Introduction by Professor Stephen Mennell

Untold Stories is a fascinating collection of personal stories by and about Protestants in the Republic of Ireland. The book demonstrates that there is a great diversity of voices to be found amongst the Protestant community. The stereotype of a privileged, aloof class, loyal to England, is shown to be largely myth. Most of the contributors are fiercely proud of their Irish heritage, while remaining critical of many aspects of the country's development over the last eighty years.

However, *Untold Stories* shows a remarkably positive outlook amongst the minority community. The contributors are drawn from all arenas of Irish life and include such well-known people as David Norris, Edna Longley, Risteárd Ó Glaisne, Bruce Arnold, Hilary Wakeman and Donald Caird, among others. The contributors are generally hopeful about the changes of the last decade, whilst recognising the many challenges that lie ahead for their community and country.

€21.50 (plus €2.50 postage) • ISBN 1-904148-14-X • paperback
Published October 2002 • 250 pages

To order, telephone The Liffey Press at (01) 8511458.
Visa and Mastercard accepted. Orders shipped within 24 hours.

Or send a cheque to The Liffey Press, Ashbrook House,
10 Main Street, Raheny, Dublin 5.

www.theliffeypress.com

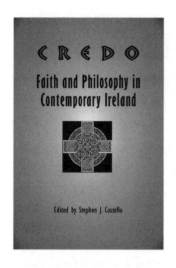